Secrets to …

Surviving the Marriage Fog

Why marriages suffer, fail, survive, and thrive

By Dr. Bob Whiddon, Jr.

Published by

Me Third!!! Publications
P.O. Box 821804
Vancouver, WA 98682

God First, Others Second, Me Third.

ISBN: 978-0-615-36698-2

Cover Design and Page Layout by NosyRoseDesigns
Lynn M. Snyder - NosyRoseDesigns@gmail.com

Dedication

I first and foremost thank God for this book.
It is His wisdom throughout these pages.

I dedicate this book to my wife, Debbie, who has been
my partner in life for over 33 years. She is my wife,
my love, my partner, and my best friend.

I also dedicate this book to my children:
Krista, who will celebrate her first anniversary this year;
Bobby, who will celebrate his 7th anniversary this year;
and Matthew, who will get married someday.

Special thanks go out to my friends who took the time
to read my book and do a lot of editing for me.
Thanks to Debbie Whiddon, Deb Hubbell,
Bonnie Miller, Rich & Jane Kolb.

TABLE OF CONTENTS

PART I

The Fog

The View from the Fog

I HATE DRIVING IN FOG. It just messes everything up. I'm the type of driver who wants to get to my destination as quickly as possible. Like when we host a marriage workshop on the Oregon Coast. If there is no traffic, we should be able to get from our home in Vancouver, Washington, to the designated hotel in one hour and 45 minutes. So, for one thing, we leave when the traffic won't delay my preplanned schedule. The schedule is not publicized anywhere except in my mind, which makes for some heated discussions and arguments with my wife when she doesn't honor the schedule—you know—the one I dreamed up in my head but didn't tell her about. So we get onto the road and head into downtown Portland where we are supposed to get on the coast highway. It's always crowded in Portland, but we usually choose a time that makes it a bit less congested. So we dart off onto Highway 26, the coast highway (they call it the Sunset Highway) right on schedule to get there in just one hour and 45 minutes. We do okay for about 10 miles, going freeway speeds, until we hit the Coast Range, those inconvenient mountains between me and my destination. It's not bad enough to have to deal with two-lane traffic, slower speeds, and even slower drivers that seem to always be in front of me. More times than not we get bogged down in fog. There is so much moisture in the air in the Pacific Northwest that fog is often a problem.

On this particular night no one was in front of me, well at least not after I passed that last slowpoke on the uphill passing lane. But after cresting the hill we ran into a thick fog. Oh great, there goes the schedule! I had to slow down because I couldn't see more than 100 feet in front of me. So for the next hour I cautiously steered through many curves in the road, passing driveways and forest roads that popped up out of nowhere. I knew there were small towns along the way and a few stores and gas stations, but we glimpsed them only as we passed them. I hated not knowing where I was going. I mean, I knew where I was going or where I wanted to go. But the fog made it impossible to see if the road ahead was straight or curved, free of danger or filled with broken tree limbs, potholes, or a wandering deer. And there was no beauty at all in this drive. Ordinarily, the drive on the Sunset Highway from Portland to the Oregon Coast is beautiful, at least for those of you who drive slow enough to enjoy the scenery. But not for me. Especially not on this trip.

The more I drove the more frustrated I became. The more frustrated I became, the more my wife noticed. And the more my wife noticed the more vocal she became about my driving. And the more vocal she became, the more vocal I became. Why won't she just keep quiet? I don't want to be all frustrated for my marriage workshop where I tell couples how to communicate well and have a happy …

Well, you can see that the fog made me behave improperly towards my wife. But it wasn't the fog that made me do anything. Here's what really happened: because of the fog, because I couldn't see clearly, because things weren't progressing as well as I had hoped they would, and because my wife offered negative critiques, I made the decision to behave badly. My bad choices were made because life around me had suddenly become foggy.

I suppose it was good that we were on our way to a marriage workshop. When I came to my senses, I apologized to my wife and we worked through the conflict using the same process that I teach couples at the workshop. We kissed and made up and had a great drive, through the fog, to the hotel.

My simple story shows so clearly the problem that most couples go through early in their marriage. There is a "marriage fog" that creeps in at different times in marriage. Some marriages see the fog earlier, some marriages see it later. But for the most part, the third or fourth year of marriages are the foggiest. Unclear eyes and misunderstanding hearts make for serious arguments. And, because the couple can't see their way out of the fog, they believe there is nothing else they can do. Divorce seems the only way out. This happens too many times.

There is an epidemic of divorce in America today. Recent statistics indicate that half of all first marriages end in divorce. And of those marriages that will end in divorce, most of them end in the third or fourth year of marriage. They get into the fog and don't know what to do, except to divorce. Divorce, for many, seems to be the best solution to the foggy marriage.

There is another statistic out there. It is well known that for those couples who live together before they marry, there is a greater chance they will divorce. Their divorce rate is higher than the 50 percent of the couples that don't live together before marriage. And here's the interesting thing- of those couples who live together before marriage, most will get married in the third or fourth year of living together. They, like those first time married couples, enter the fog and don't know what to do. But for them divorce is not an option because they are not married. So they do the opposite. Marriage seems to be the best solution for the foggy live-in arrangement. These couples believe that marriage will get them to the next level, whatever that is. The marriage certificate will recharge their stale relationship. The wedding will fix what's broken. So, already in the fog, they marry and stay in the fog. Not much changes. And, with less patience for one another than those married couples that did not live together before marriage, they believe divorce is now the best solution for a foggy marriage. After all, they tried living together without a marriage. Then they tried marriage to fix their foggy relationship. So when the fog didn't lift, divorce was the only way out.

Steve and Janice came in for counseling one day. I told them what I tell every couple: "Start wherever you want and tell me why you're here." They began to tell me a story of love, true love that they had for each other. They want to get married but wanted me to help them understand if this was the right decision. They had been married before, to one another, and just six months ago they had a quickie divorce using on-line advice and proper forms. He moved out, she went on with her life. But just a month after their mail-in divorce was finalized, they realized they had made a mistake. They were both deeply in love with each other. She even tried to go out with another man after the divorce. All she could think about was the man she just pushed out of her home, out of her life. But he was a drinker. He didn't care about what it did to the family…at least until he had to leave his home. He got into rehab, a 12-step program, and a church. He drastically changed. He became the man his wife had wanted all the time. So now, only six months after they had divorced, they were asking me if it was too early to get remarried.

I started to ask my "counselor" questions. You know, just to get a better picture of what was really going on with them. I asked, "How long were you married? "Four years," she said. "I just couldn't take all the problems." Hmm, four years. I found out she had been married twice before. "Tell me about your previous marriage," I asked. She began, "Well, I was pregnant so it didn't start like I wanted, but we were happy, for a while. I filed divorce papers one time because he wouldn't stop lying to me and taking drugs and drinking. That seemed to get him to straighten up for a while." I interrupted, "How long were you married before you filed divorce papers? She thought for a moment and said, "I guess we were married for three or, um, maybe four years." Hmm, four years? She continued to describe how he changed when all of their problems came to a head. And things were better for a while. "Then after a while he went back to his old ways," she continued. "Then we finally divorced after about 8 years." Well I did the quick math. Their marriage almost ended after four years, but an ultimatum sparked their marriage to last another four years before a final divorce. Hmm, four years. Then I asked about her first marriage. It began with a teenage pregnancy, lasted about three years, and then they divorced. Steve had also been married twice before. Both of his first two marriages ended after three or four years. Living in the marriage fog they could not see their own dysfunctional relationship patterns. When I mentioned that all of their relationships lasted three or four years, Janice gasped. She had never seen the pattern.

Another couple, Bill and Mary, came in for counseling. They said they needed help in communicating. "We just can't talk to one another," Mary said. "He shuts down when we talk. He says I criticize him all the time. I just want him to see the big picture. But he won't talk to me for days, weeks sometimes!" I was listening to a description of a normal marriage. This kind of thing happens to most couples on some level. So, I started asking more probing questions to get the big picture. They had been married for 11 years. "Was it always this bad?" I asked. "No, we started out very much in love and had a great time," Bill chimed in. "So," I asked, "when did you notice that things started changing?" They both looked at one another. "About the third or fourth year, I imagine," Mary answered. Bill shook his head in agreement. There it was again, three or four years. They had entered the marriage fog, that third or fourth year fog. But instead of divorce, they decided to live unhappily ever after, at least until they decided to come to me for help.

The three-year fog in marriage is a pattern in every marriage. And because it's a fog, where couples can't see clearly enough to see what's really happening, they try things that are not productive. The fog claims more marriages.

Stories of the fog are all around me. A young couple I know married right after high school and went out of state to begin their new life together. I saw her the other day, but not him. They are no longer married, after about three years.

Another couple I know were both professionals, she working at a college, he managing a store. They seemed to have good heads on their shoulders. Both were in their mid-twenties when they married which statistically gives the marriage a greater chance of succeeding. But after about three years, they called it quits.

As I am writing this chapter a young man calls to set up a counseling appointment with me. It seems that he has been living with his girlfriend for a while. They have a 15-month old child. "My ex kicked me out of the house the other day," he explained. It did not surprise me that he called her his "ex" even though there was no formal marriage. To cohabiting couples, the live-in relationship is just as real as most of us experience in marriage. But then I started to do some quick math. Let's see, a 15-month old child plus nine months to make that child, this couple has been together for at least two years. Which means they may be in their third or fourth year together. We set an appointment for the following day, but before hanging up the phone I asked, "How long have you and your girlfriend been together?" "Oh, about three and a half years." Hmmmmmm.

All of us know friends and family members who have divorced. Go back and see how long their marriages lasted. Many of them, you'll be sad when you realize, ended after three or four years. And, how about your own marriage? Try to remember what it was like in the third or fourth year. Most of you reading this book will have to admit that you can see it. The fog was there. You both changed because of it. Many of you still have problems in your marriage because of what happened during the fog.

I can remember my own marriage. The third and fourth years were definitely bad. There were other factors that didn't help matters much. I had just graduated from college with a bachelor's degree and headed off to my first ministry. We moved from Lubbock, Texas, a nice-sized town of about 100,000 at that time, to Los Angeles, California, a little bit bigger town of over 8,000,000. We lived in The Valley, the San Fernando Valley, in the area called Van Nuys. It was 107 degrees on that August day that we drove to our new home. There were fires in the hills on three sides of the valley. Ash fell on our home and car like snowflakes. The smog was outrageous. And there we were, ready to minister. I poured my heart into the ministry, to the neglect of my wife. She poured her heart into baby-sitting and foster care. Her greatest need was and is social interaction and friendship, both of which I had denied her. So she went her way (emotionally) and I went mine. It was a pattern that would be the norm for the next six or seven years of our marriage. But we didn't know what had gone wrong. The marriage fog rolled in. Instead of correcting the problems, we went into survival mode. We ignored each other's true needs. Now, don't get me wrong, we got along for the most part. We still enjoyed intimacy. She was still a great part of my ministry, a support for what I felt I had to do. But it wasn't the Cinderella marriage I thought we would have. When our kids came along I felt we were good parents. But something was missing. Something big.

I remember going to marriage classes, even teaching some myself. I remember hearing other couples claiming, "He/she is my best friend." They would speak of sharing their lives, in loving and happy ways, with one another. I didn't have that. I even wondered if I could ever tell my wife that she was my best friend. I couldn't.

After we had been married about 14 years, we felt called to open our home to a 16-year old boy whose parents could no longer keep him in their home. It was an intense situation. He was in our home for three years. One time we had to call the police because we found several thousands of dollars worth of band equipment in our home that he had stolen from the local high school. The stress of dealing with this boy brought our marriage to the breaking point. He finally left on his own. But our marriage was suffering. All those marriage problems could be traced back to those poor decisions we made when the fog rolled in.

In the meantime, I had entered a Ph.D. program in pastoral counseling. As a minister I was faced with many people who believed I had answers to their life's problems. It was a good decision to get that degree. I centered in on marriage issues as my "specialty." And, as I counseled with couples whose marriages were falling apart, I noticed that all of them had the same problems. The details were different in the marriages, but the issues were the same. All couples got to the point they couldn't hold a decent conversation with each other. They had gotten to the point where they could not resolve any problem no matter how small. They had gotten to the point of despising one another, even to the point of hatred. But I also discovered that most marriages started going bad in the third and fourth year. And, since I knew what had gone wrong during that time, I was able to give tools to help couples communicate and resolve conflicts. That's why I am writing this book. I know the secret. I know when most marriages start having trouble. I know why the trouble comes. And I know how to repair the marriage. Keep reading and you'll know the secret, too.

Well, back to my marriage. Even with a Ph.D. and the ability to help other couples regain the love they had at the beginning of their marriage, I still went home to a mediocre marriage. Then one night I had an epiphany. Well, it was a realization of how stupid I was. I had never put into practice what I told other couples to do. I had a beautiful wife. She had put up with me for many years. She didn't leave me when she should have. She wasn't treating me like garbage, though I wasn't treating her with the love she deserved. I loved her, but I didn't like her very much. All of our problems, at this time, could again be traced back to the fog that invaded our young marriage, in the third year, when we adapted instead of attacking the problems.

I remember clearly the night that I decided to put into practice the things I demanded my clients to do. I knew if they did those things they would fall in love all over again. So I started. Everyday I did what a good husband should do even if his wife does not reciprocate. I remember it took an entire year, twelve months. But I woke up one day and realized that I had the most wonderful wife I could ever have hoped for. Our intimacy had grown. Our sex-life was awesome. Our outlook was fantastic. We had fallen in love all over again. And, I could finally say without hesitation, she was my best friend. She IS my best friend.

The marriage fog had claimed us, too. Because we didn't understand what was going on, we short-circuited our marriage. We adapted to the problems rather than fixing them.

Today, we can see clearly. We understand the marriage fog. We know what it looks like and how it hurts marriages. And we also know how to help people out of the fog. My wife and I spend over 25 weeks every year teaching married couples how to have a healthier and happier marriage. We teach intensive one-day workshops in retreat settings. We teach in weekend workshops at local churches. And we teach once-a-week classes for eight to ten weeks. And most of what we do is open people's eyes to what's been going on. Once their eyes are open, the solutions to marriage problems are simple.

The third or fourth year is not the only time fog rolls into a marriage. They used to say that couples go through a "seven-year itch" or a time when there was a natural downturn in the mood of the marriage. Made popular by Marilyn Monroe's movie with the same title, Americans in the 1950s and 1960s braced themselves for that seventh year when things might go awry. But that seven-year itch was just an extension of that third or fourth year fog. Back then, societal norms and religious pressures kept couples together longer. Even if love faded, the commitment to keep the marriage together, whether it was loveless or not, was important. In November of 2007 a study came out that claimed the "'Seven-year itch' now five." The article suggested that marital commitment faded from the 1950s to the present because of America's love affair with instant gratification. They no longer felt the need to keep a loveless marriage together, opting more for new and exciting adventures. The seven-year itch, well the five-year itch, is really that same early fog that claims most couples.

There is another fog that hits marriages around the twenty-year mark. In fact, this is the fastest growing group of divorces in America today. It may be explained by the empty-nest syndrome that hits these marriages. The kids grow up and leave home. The husband and wife, because they spent all their time and energies on the kids to the neglect of the marriage, find that they have nothing in common. They have no skills in communication. And, they may have no desire to rekindle what has long died. So, because they don't know what to do, the fog consumes and destroys them. Even if couples in this category don't divorce, many will limp along unhappily for the rest of their lives.

The marriage fog is real. The statistics describing the troubles in the third and fourth year of marriage are real. Problems facing empty nesters are real. In the next chapter we will explain why the fog comes and how it affects you. In the following chapters we will tell you all about the fog, show you how to fix the damage the fog brings, and how to have a happy and healthy marriage for the rest of your life.

My wife and I have been married for 33 years now. We are having a blast. And every year gets better and better. We believe that every marriage problem can be resolved and every marriage can be saved! We are living proof.

How the Fog Forms

FOG USUALLY ROLLS IN. But most of the time we don't have the luxury of watching it actually roll. I do remember that football game, the one they call the Fog Bowl, played on December 31, 1988. It was a playoff game between the Philadelphia Eagles and the Chicago Bears. All of America was watching. The cameras captured the low-lying clouds rolling towards the stadium. Then, in the second quarter of this nationally televised game, the fog consumed the stadium. Those of us watching TV couldn't see the whole field. And when a pass was thrown, we never saw the ball. It was amazing that the game continued. The Bears won 20-12.

Weathermen can predict fog. It usually rolls in. But in our part of the world, we don't see it roll. We usually wake up to a fully fog-consumed metropolis. Then we scramble to adapt, whether we have to walk to a bus stop or school, or whether we have to navigate the freeways towards our place of business. In this case, the fog is just there. For most, we don't really know how it got there or when it will leave. We just adapt and try to survive the dreary foggy day.

The marriage fog also rolls in. Those of us who have studied the phenomenon know where it originates and how it rolls slowly into all marriages. But for most couples, they wake up one morning and POW! they're in the middle of it. So they adapt, accept the false notion that they can't do anything about it, and limp along until, someday, the fog just goes away. But the fog doesn't go away. Or, at least, that's how it feels.

Well, enough talk about weather and stuff. Let's talk about marriage. Keep reading and you will find out when the fog comes, why it comes, AND how to clear it up after it consumes your marriage. Ready?

Discovering *Pure* Love

Our brains were designed to secrete chemicals that would produce a natural high when we "fall in love." We really don't "fall" at all. We experience a buzz that may last from 18 months to three years. But the euphoric feeling of love isn't the best part. It's what the feeling of love makes us do. It makes us want to "do stuff for one another." So, suddenly you are not only "in love" but you are "practicing" pure love.

There is a whole science out there devoted to the "chemistry of love." Innumerable articles and books have been written about this natural phenomenon that accompanies "falling in love." Look at this list of the chemicals that stimulate the neurons in our brains and the cells in our bodies. (*The Chemistry of Love. HowStuffWorks, Inc. http://people.howstuffworks.com/love.htm*)

- Dopamine ... to cause sexual fantasy.
- Epinephrine and Norepinephrine ... cause the heart to beat faster, making us excited.
- Serotonin ... fighting depression. Sex causes an increase of serotonin which gives a person feelings of pleasure and happiness.
- Phenylethylamine (PEA) ... associated with the feeling of well-being and romance.
- Estrogen ... causes desire and helps keep the sex drive healthy for both sexes.
- Testosterone ... responsible for the feelings of desire.
- Nitric Oxide (NO) ... increases blood flow and vessel dilation, which helps in arousal and sexual intercourse.
- Pheromones ... natural scents produced by the body and emitted through sweat pores, causing subconscious sexual attraction and desire.
- Alpha Melanocyte Polypeptide (AMP) ... associated with male erections and a male's interest in sex.

- Oxytocin … key to human bonding and love, also causes female pelvic contractions during orgasm.
- Vasoactive Intestinal Polypeptide (VIP) … essentially the same effects as nitric oxide.

Some say it's the phenylethylamine (PEA) that may last up to three years in the brain. It's also found in chocolate. That's why we connect chocolate with romance and desire.

Most of these chemicals have been manufactured and can be purchased by prescription. But none of the manufactured chemicals can do what the naturally secreted chemicals can do—make you feel so good about another person that you want to "do stuff for each other."

Pure love is wonderful and exciting. The first year or two of any relationship is smothered in pure love. Couples, even teenage couples, constantly think of what they can do for each other. It's a great lifestyle … while it lasts. Remember the fog?

Here's what *really* happens

No more beating around the bush. Here's what actually happens. STEP ONE—YOU FALL (in love). STEP TWO— YOU DO (acts of service for each other). Remember what the "love high" made you do. It made it fun and pleasurable to "do stuff for each other." You unknowingly became a servant, taking care of the needs of the other with amazing consistency and energy. Then, STEP THREE—YOU ENJOY (the good feelings after you serve). These are the three distinct steps in relationships that included true love. But keep them separate. True love is "doing stuff" while the other two steps are just feelings.

But between 18-months to three-years after the initial "love high" the chemicals begin to fade. Now as the chemicals wear off, it's not so pleasurable to do stuff for each other. We wake up one morning and begin to think, "You know, I'm giving a whole lot more to this relationship than I'm getting …"

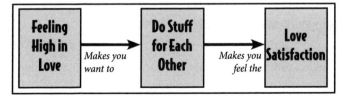

At this point I begin to back off from the whole servant thing. My wife wakes up one morning and notices my lack of care, and she begins to think, "You know, I'm giving a whole lot more to this relationship than I'm getting …" So she starts backing off. We now have a gap in our marriage. And everyday that we possess the attitude of "getting" instead of "giving," the gap widens. It's no longer fun to serve, so we quit serving or "doing stuff for each other."

Most of us never knew that we were initially experiencing a high. It not only gave us the good feeling of love, but it made us feel even better when we served. That's when true love happens. I suppose that was the first bit of fog—the not knowing—but we didn't care because we were so in love. And love worked. It worked well.

Well … now another bank of fog rolls into our marriage. Again, it's because we don't know what's going on. We know that after a while, after about two or three years, love doesn't feel as good as it used to. We believe the one we married isn't as loving as he/she used to be. But we don't know why.

Imaginary scenarios begin to invade our minds. "She stopped loving me." "He doesn't care about me any more." "She's destroying our marriage." "If he would do what he's supposed to do our marriage would be better." "If she's not gonna do this, then I'm not gonna to do that." On and on the accusations go. Some of them verbal, most of them imagined. The crucial fact that hasn't come to mind is that there is no healthy communication going on at all. With no communication, there is no intimacy (closeness). With no intimacy there is no desire to work things out. With no desire to work things out, there is nothing left. So couples do the only thing they think they know how to do—end their marriage. After all, he's the one who won't change. She's the one who won't change. The fog consumes and destroys another marriage.

Here's what *really, really* happens

Are you ready for an epiphany? Remember what I'm about to say. Write it down. Memorize it. Because this very problem will come up again. Here's what really, really happened:

When the chemical high wore off, YOU changed from selfless to selfish, from servant to miser!

The whole time you were doing stuff for that one you loved, the "doing" was what made you feel good. Doing good things for others always makes you feel good. The chemicals just made you WANT to do it more.

So now you are turning away from your mate and concentrating on yourself, what you're not getting, what you think you deserve. Anytime you focus on yourself you will be miserable. Think about it. No matter what the other person does, it won't be good enough, it won't be done exactly right or at the exact right time, and it won't be done often enough to truly please you. Focusing on you will always be frustrating. But focusing on someone else will always be physically, emotionally, mentally, and spiritually satisfying.

God's Word told us a long time ago that we would be frustrated if we focused on self. "What is the source of every quarrel and conflict among you? Is it not your pleasures that wage war in your members? … You are envious and cannot obtain; so you fight and quarrel" *(James 4:1-2)*. Anytime we decide to think more of ourselves than others, there will be a natural tendency to fight. What we're really doing is trying to push the other down so we can feel good. Not a good way of handling life, or marriage.

The Simple Solution

I suppose, if you want, you can throw the book away after you read this next small section. I'm about to tell you everything you need to know to fix any problem in your marriage. Well, don't THROW the book away. Give it to someone else to read it.

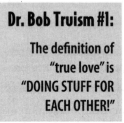

Dr. Bob Truism #1:

The definition of "true love" is "DOING STUFF FOR EACH OTHER!"

Remember the Dr. Bob Truism #1— The "high in love" feeling made you want to serve, but it was the act of serving that caused you to experience true love. Now, with those naturally secreted brain chemicals wearing off, the "high in love" feeling is no longer there to motivate you to serve. From now on, you must decide to serve. The "high" wasn't true love, anyway. TRUE LOVE is the result of serving. So, you don't feel much like serving? Tough! Get to work.

But, when you serve, the satisfaction of TRUE LOVE will overwhelm you. This is the solution. This isn't rocket science. It's marriage. It should be simple for two loving people to love each other. Get to work! Start serving again.

The California Self-Esteem Project

There are two major studies that have proven a positive connection between behavior and feelings, if done in the right order. Many used to believe you cannot do good things if you do not feel good. So, let's stop everything and wait until we feel good. This has been disproved—big time.

The first study was the infamous California Self-Esteem Project. In 1986 a group of California legislators convinced themselves that low self-esteem was the cause of a myriad of behavioral problems in school, including poor school performance. The group appropriated $750,000 to help educators raise the self-esteem of school students in hopes that this would increase school performance as well as lower the rates of juvenile misbehavior. The test was an utter failure.

The premise of the study was that working on self-esteem would improve behavior. They worked on feelings in hopes that this would automatically increase responsibility. The California Task Force to Promote Self-Esteem and Personal and Social Responsibility published their findings in a book called *The Social Importance of Self-Esteem.* A *USA Today* article described the results in this way:

> THE EDITORS MIGHT AS WELL HAVE TITLED IT THE SOCIAL UNIMPORTANCE OF SELF-ESTEEM BECAUSE THEY FOUND PRACTICALLY NO CONNECTION BETWEEN SELF-ESTEEM AND ANY OF THE BEHAVIORS THEY STUDIED. AS NIEL SMELSER NOTED IN THE INTRODUCTION, "ONE OF THE DISAPPOINTING ASPECTS OF EVERY CHAPTER IN THIS VOLUME ... IS HOW THE LOW ASSOCIATIONS BETWEEN SELF-ESTEEM AND ITS CONSEQUENCES ARE IN RESEARCH TO DATE." OVER THE YEARS, OTHER REVIEWERS HAVE OFFERED SIMILAR READINGS OF THE AVAILABLE RESEARCH, POINTING OUT THE RESULTS ARE UNIMPRESSIVE OR CHARACTERIZED BY MASSIVE INCONSISTENCIES AND CONTRADICTIONS. THE CALIFORNIA TASK FORCE WAS NOT A DISINTERESTED GROUP OF SCHOLARS. THEY WANTED TO FIND A LINK. NEVERTHELESS, WHEN THEIR RESEARCH FAILED TO TURN ONE UP, THEY HAD THE HONESTY TO ADMIT IT. (*USA TODAY,* JAN, 1998, BY NINA H. SHOKRAII)

This has always been the way behavior and feelings have worked. Good behavior must happen because it's the right thing to do. But when it's done, the good feelings naturally follow. Behavior must come before feelings. For too many years people thought the other way, that a person had to feel good to do good things. Well, that didn't work. We are finally getting to understand that good behavior brings on the good feelings. You must decide to serve!

This same solution is what God gave to Cain in one

of the first stories in the Bible. God asked Cain and his brother, Abel, to offer a blood sacrifice to Him. Abel did what God requested. But Cain offered a sacrifice of "fruit of the ground." God did not appreciate Cain's disobedience. Cain went off—depressed. So, God went to Cain and asked, "Why are you angry? And why has your face fallen?" (Genesis 4:6) The word "face" in that verse has to do with one's entire demeanor. Cain was depressed! But God did not give Cain time to answer His question. Instead, God gave Cain the answer: "If you do what is right, will not your face lift up?" (verse 7) God's prescription for the blues, not feeling good about yourself, was not to work on your feelings. Rather, God demanded that Cain DO what was right. But the natural consequence for DOING was FEELING GOOD. Again, this has always been the case. We are required to do right no matter how we feel at the moment. But God has always promised that the good feelings will follow our right actions.

The Mother Teresa Effect

The second major study linking feelings and behavior was a study that resulted in the discovery of the "Mother Teresa Effect." In the 1980s a disease called AIDS invaded our country. The HIV virus attacked the victim's immune system so it could no longer fight off diseases. Those living with AIDS usually died of something that most of us could normally fight off, like pneumonia. Medical science worked at finding not only medicine to fight the virus, but also finding something that could boost or strengthen the immune system. Harvard Medical School researcher, Dr. David McClelland, took a group of students and had them watch film clips of Mother Teresa taking care of the sick and dying in Calcutta, India. The researcher took samples of the student's saliva before and after viewing the film clips. He found that the immune system increased in strength. The phrase "The Mother Teresa Effect" was coined. Many schools of medicine and schools of psychology have repeated this experiment with the same result. Others have discovered even more health benefits of doing acts of kindness.

In applying this to marriage, it seems to be a no-brainer. If you focus on self you will always be disappointed and miserable. But if you focus on the needs of another, like your wife or husband, you will always increase in health. That's why married people live longer, get sick less often, and enjoy life more. The solution, then, to recapture the feelings of love and excitement about being in a relationship is to serve.

Servanthood *vs.* Slavery

We need to be careful at this point to understand the difference between servanthood and slavery. Too many times a well-meaning husband or wife will think, "Well, I guess there's nothing we can do about our problems so I guess I'll just do whatever he wants, put all my feelings aside, and let him have his way." This is a person who has put herself into a position of slavery. She is giving up on the marriage (not good). She thinks that her feelings are no longer important or valid (not good). And she thinks that letting her husband have his way in all matters is the only way to have a good marriage (very not good).

That's the inherent problem in slavery. A person does not get to choose what he/she wants to do. Feelings are not allowed. Work is demanded. Someone else rules over your time, energy, goals, and dreams. And if I remember right, slavery was outlawed in this country years ago. It wasn't good then and it's not good today.

So let's use another word to describe a more healthy relationship in marriage. I have chosen the word servanthood. Here's my definition:

- I get to choose to be a servant
- I get to choose to ignore those little things she does that used to irritate me

- As a servant, I get to choose what I do, when I do it, how long I do it, and how often I do it
- I get to do these acts of kindness without expecting anything in return
- I get to do these acts of kindness whether my mate deserves them or not

Here are some benefits of choosing to be a servant:
- I become more healthy (The Mother Teresa Effect)
- I have less stress in my life because I don't have to worry about myself
- I have more energy because I get to choose when to serve
- I get to be involved in the things that make my mate happy

The biggest benefit to a lifestyle of serving is this: My mate becomes more beautiful everyday! What? That's right, my mate becomes more beautiful every day that I choose to serve her/him. And it's all because you changed your attitude towards your mate.

Think about a Hollywood marriage. Some hunky specimen of maleness marries the top lingerie model in America. It seems destined to go down in history as one of the greatest romances of all-time, next to "Cinderella" or "Sleeping Beauty." But within a year the couple splits up.

The paparazzi interview both and find that they hate each other. They are saying all kinds of disgusting things about each other. We ordinary people are thinking, "Are you kidding me? He doesn't want her anymore? That beauty? Is he crazy?" The women are thinking the same thing about the crazy woman who doesn't want that hunky man any more. So, what changed? Did they both stop being

Dr. Bob Truism #2:

Sex, outside of a growing intimate relationship, gets VERY BORING, VERY QUICKLY!

beautiful? Did they both change? Neither changed, except in attitude. With no communication, the couple quickly drifts apart. But they are surprised at how the other changed from being a "dream come true" to a "nightmare gone wrong." He chose to look at her with disgust. She did the same. And when you make this choice, the other person becomes uglier every day.

Your attitude towards your mate makes him/her, in your own mind, more beautiful or more ugly every day. So, it's up to you. But what most of us do, you know, when the chemical high fades, is to dwell on the negative. That's the fog. That's why it just rolls in. If you don't understand it, it may seem like the only possible solution is divorce.

But now that you have read this book this far, you know too much. You cannot plead ignorance any longer. You know that you have to change.

It won't be that bad. Keep reading and you'll see how easy it is to make the fog go away and get your marriage back to the slurpy, sloppy, sweet, kissyface, loving marriage you enjoyed in the beginning. Trust me!

PART II

Defogging Your Marriage

What is Marriage?

KNOWLEDGE IS THE KEY. If I can get you to understand what marriage is really about and how it's supposed to work, half of all your problems will disappear I guarantee it!

The reason that marriage is a fog for most people is because they don't understand what marriage is or what they will be expected to do to make the marriage work. Each of us has our fantasies about marriage. The Cinderella syndrome makes us all believe that once we enter that "hallowed state of bliss" we will all live happily ever after. NOT! That's what's wrong with the Cinderella-esque stories in our world. They end at the wedding, but they don't show us what life is like after the "I Do" confessions. So we create visions of marriage based on the wedding, and the honeymoon, and other wonderful romantic scenes we watch in the movies, with the perfect kiss, with perfect words, and with a full orchestra in the background playing perfect music.

Jane wakes up the morning after the wedding. Vivid memories of a perfect wedding fill her head. The night of romance, intimacy, and passion has left a big smile on her face. She sits up in bed, straightens her negligee, tucks the sheets and blankets around her, and lovingly awaits the breakfast her husband will make for her and serve to her before her feet ever hit the floor. It's an honest expectation, for she came from a family in which her father did this for her mother. John awakes to his beautiful bride sitting with great anticipation. He too arranges the pillows, sheets and blankets, with excited expectation to receive a homemade breakfast in bed that his new wife will bring. For he was raised in a home in which his mother often did this for his father. Do you see a problem here? Do you see the fog beginning to roll in?

No matter what you call your fantasies or how you describe them, they all have one thing in common—selfishness. We enter marriage with selfish expectations! We, as single people, have developed a lifestyle of self-serving. We do what we want to do, what makes us happy, what is pleasurable to us. Our self-serving attitude influences our choice of jobs, restaurants at which we eat, hobbies that occupy our free time, and yes, even the girl or boy we look for and find. We look at all these things with the idea of "what do I get out of it?"

Right now you are either surprised at the new knowledge you are gaining about marriage, or you are mad at me for suggesting you entered marriage with selfish motives. Well don't be surprised or mad at me. You didn't know. You were high, remember? The feeling of love that we experienced made us do what we were supposed to do—serve the other person. It was almost like we "accidentally" did what was right at the beginning of the relationship. And when we served the other person, we experienced true love satisfaction. It was a great cycle, as long as the "high" lasted. But when the high wore off, we reverted to living an expecting lifestyle rather than a giving lifestyle.

So, now you've been married for one or two years and it seems like things aren't like they're supposed to be. But on what do you base your ideas of "what's supposed to be?" You base them on your fantasies about marriage. We've now gone full circle back to selfishness.

This is why the fog comes in—we don't understand what marriage is supposed to be. This is why we divorce so quickly in the third or fourth year—we don't understand why AND we don't know what to do to correct the problems.

ENOUGH IS ENOUGH! It's time to defog your marriage with knowledge. So, one more time, let's ask: "What is marriage supposed to look like?"

Marriage Completes You!

If you care about what *The Designer* of marriages said, read this:

> *Then the Lord God said, "It is not good for man to be alone; I will make him a helper suitable for him ..."* (GENESIS 2:18)

Suitable? Not the best English word for the true meaning there. The literal translation of that word is closer to "corresponding to the need." The Designer designed the woman to fill the emptiness that was designed into the man. So, woman was designed to complete the man, and vice versa. They were both designed to actively, pro-actively take care of the needs of the other.

If you don't care what The Designer of marriages said, don't write it off as religious legend. It's still true, and it has been proven to be true in modern, social research studies. Read here what a modern researcher said about the benefits of marriage. Dr. Linda Waite, in her book *A Case for Marriage: Why Married People are Happier, Healthier, and Better Off Financially* (Broadway Books, paperback 2001), lists proven benefits that married people enjoy over single people. A few of these are:

- Marriage lowers the risk that both men and women will become victims of violence

- Married people live longer
- Children lead healthier, longer lives if parents get and stay married
- Married men make more money than single men
- On average, married people retire with over twice the assets that single people have
- Marriage increases sexual fidelity
- Married men and women are less depressed, less anxious, and less psychologically distressed than single, divorced or widowed Americans
- Almost twice as many married people than single people rate their lives as "very happy"
- Divorce weakens the bonds between parents and children over the long run
- Married people are more likely to report that they have an extremely satisfying sex life than are single people or those that live together without marriage

So, how do you explain this? Could it be that unmarried people are missing something important in their lives? Men, did you know that research has proven that marriage offers more benefits to the man than the woman?

Whoa, that sure sounds like a lot of benefits. If we're not careful, we could look at this selfishly—as more things that I can get out of marriage. Before reverting to your old ways, read the next section to catch a glimpse of what you're supposed to do in your marriage.

Marriage Unites Two Human Beings

What have you heard at weddings? "Union of two spirits." "United in Holy Matrimony." "What God hath joined together let no man put asunder." What?!? What do you picture when someone mentions marital unity? It's hard to imagine, unless the marriage goes bad. Then images like "the old ball and chain" come into place.

How about this image: Marriage, the ultimate blended family? When you marry, you and your mate become a whole new entity. It's kind of like when you mix colors. If you mix black and white it becomes gray. The black and white are no longer visible. The only thing that remains is a new color. If you mix yellow and blue you get green. At this exact moment, as I am writing this chapter, I am wearing a green shirt. I'm looking down and can't see any blue or yellow. But I know the green in my shirt is a mixture of two primary colors that have now disappeared into one new color.

How about this image: Marriage unifies two bodies? That may not be such a good image. It's more like science fiction with a two-headed, four-armed, and four-legged creature unleashed on the countryside.

But, try to put all these images together. Two humans, united in marriage, blended so much that they become a whole new entity. Marriage is supposed to "glue" you so tightly to your mate that we can't tell where one person ends and the other begins. Your mate becomes an extension of you—your body, your mind, and your spirit.

Now, think SURVIVAL. If my hand gets close to a fire, I will naturally recoil and keep my hand at a safe distance. If I get hungry, I will search for nourishment to calm the hunger pangs. If I desire pleasure, I will consider the needs of my body and pursue appropriate stimuli. All of these things I will do as a matter of survival. It's the natural thing to do.

Now, transfer all these thoughts, feelings, and actions over to your mate. In marriage you must treat your mate as an extension of yourself. If he/she hurts, you hurt with him/her. If there is danger, you will protect your mate as you would your own self. And if pleasure is desired, thoughts of what your mate needs should be just as important, even more important, than your own needs.

If you care about what The Designer of marriage said about love, true love, read what He said through the writer Paul:

> *So husbands ought to love their own wives as their own bodies. He who loves his own wife loves himself. For no one ever hated his own body, but nourishes and cherishes it ...* (EPHESIANS 5:28-29)

When you married, you volunteered to spend more energy on your mate's life than your own. When you serve your mate, you enjoy the blessings because he/she is actually a part of you. How's that working for you? Social and medical research shows us this is healthy. Serving the needs of your spouse has been proven to make you happier and more satisfied with life. That's what you signed up for. That's what marriage looks like.

No Longer Single, but a Couple

When you got married you gave up life as a single, selfish person and volunteered to live as part of a couple. Your vocabulary should have changed. Words like me, myself and I should have been replaced with us, ours, and we. When you gave up your single life for the healthier married life, you also gave up rights to expect or demand things your own way. You volunteered to replace selfishness with selflessness.

Jack and Nancy received a fantastic present at their wedding. His mother deeded over his boyhood home to the new couple. It seemed like a good thing, but turned out to be a disaster. Nancy moved in and began to arrange the areas of the home that she thought she would be in charge of, like the kitchen, living room, bathrooms, master bedroom, etc. But every time she arranged things her way, Jack would go behind her and arrange things they way he remembered. He told her, "This is the home I grew up in. You can't just change things." Jack wanted to be married, but he wanted things to be the same as when he was single. His refusal to "blend" and "give" in his marriage caused many problems. The couple came to me for counseling. They had been married three years.

What do you do about holiday traditions? We can't just go to my family's home for Christmas every year, like I'm used to. I now have another family to consider. My wife and I determined early that we would go to my parents' home for Thanksgiving and her parents' home for Christmas that first year. The next year we would switch the destinations. When our kids came along, we kept that same plan and it worked well. I hated missing Christmas at my parents' home that first year, but I was married now. New traditions had to be formed in our newly formed family. Later, when we moved too far away from both parents to safely travel during the winter, we started having Thanksgiving and Christmas at our own home with some special friends.

I do remember when I first married that my wife didn't arrange our home in the way I expected. I came from a home in which we strove for the appearance of neatness. She came from a home in which they strove for the appearance of lived-in comfort. I remember my wife telling me one time, "I don't want to live in a model home. I want to be comfortable in my own home." I didn't understand her statement then. I wish I did. I would have avoided many problems. In fact, I did want to live in a model home. We butted heads. Neither of us would give in on this matter. My idea of compromise was that I would clean up my half of whatever target we argued about. So I would have nothing on my side of the dining table, coffee table, and bed. Instead, I would pile up letters, newspapers, loose change, candy wrappers, knickknacks, and anything else I considered unnecessary on her side. Well, that didn't work!

I wish I had this book when I first got married. It took me a long time to realize that my comfort and pleasure should not have been pursued. I found the more I served my wife, the happier she was, and the happier I was. Today, we don't live in a model home. But I have come to appreciate the knickknacks, plants, and decorations that make the house we live in OUR HOME.

Plans, hopes, and dreams must be shared equally by the husband and wife. Steve quit his job after about two years because he was bored. An immediate strain was put on the family that needed two incomes to make ends meet. But without talking to his wife, he walked away from a steady paycheck. Then he announced that he was going back to school to become a licensed massage therapist. He tried to convince his wife, Nancy, that this would all be better in the long run. "How could I keep going to a job that I hated?" he explained. Nancy took extra shifts at the hospital in an attempt to keep the bills current. The two years it took for Steve to finally get his license put a horrible strain on the marriage and the family. He fumbled around for a while making little money from the few clients he attracted. Six months later he quit that job with no plans for what he would do next. I have seen this story repeated many times in my years as a counselor. The husband, or the wife, thinks more of themselves than their mate or children, and limps off into one failure after another.

When we marry we give up the right to pursue only our dreams. I'm not trying to be hateful and say that you can't pursue dreams. I am saying that you cannot do it alone, without your mate. Besides, it doesn't work, it won't work. If you don't include your mate in everything that affects you, misery will enter and stay in your marriage.

Living as a Married Single

Have I already overemphasized this point in this book? Have I repeated too much how we voluntarily give up our rights to independence when we marry and choose rather to share everything with our mates? This is how happy, healthy married couples live. But, still, millions of married people, after a while, choose to live as a single in their marriage. Here's what living as a married single looks like:

- Unreasonable demands for the other to conform to one's hopes and dreams
- Separate sets of friends, defending friends over the mate if the two are ever at odds
- Separate checkbooks in which each have their separate list of obligations—no sharing!
- Separate hobbies and recreational activities, intentionally designed to keep the other from sharing this part of life
- Separate goals and dreams, all the arrangements including funding of such dreams done without sharing with the mate
- Little or no deep conversations about anything in life
- Little or no intimacy
- Little or no care or concern for the other

What a horrible turn of events. You entered marriage through a beautiful, romantic ceremony in which you promised to make each other happy for the rest of your lives. Now, you're just two married people, who don't like each other, living as singles in the same house. The fog is getting thick.

Dr. Bob Truism #3:

Marriage is the unity of two people who have voluntarily given up personal rights to voluntarily serve the needs of the other.

So, What is Marriage?

Marriage wasn't supposed to be full of pain and misery. If your life is not like you imagined it would be, keep reading to find ways to correct your situation and break through the fog. But remember what marriage is:

Marriage is the unity of two people who have voluntarily given up their personal rights to voluntarily serve the needs of the other.

As a married person, if you choose to do what is right, and what works, you will find that your mate becomes more beautiful everyday, you become more beautiful everyday, and you will become happier with each day that passes. I guarantee it!

What Does a Healthy Marriage Look Like?

KNOWLEDGE IS THE KEY! Another step in de-fogging your marriage is to understand what the goal is, or what you're working towards. Anyone can say, "I want a healthy marriage." But if you don't know what one looks like, you won't know what you're looking for, how to proceed, or how to know if you have arrived. So, what does a healthy marriage look like?

#1- IN A HEALTHY MARRIAGE, BOTH PARTNERS UNDERSTAND THAT THEY ARE DIFFERENT.

Okay, I'll be the first to admit that I don't understand my wife completely. And, she'll admit the same about me. There is no way on earth that I, as a man, will ever totally understand her. But there are many things that I do understand that makes my marriage wonderful. I understand that we're different, we talk different languages, and we look at EVERYTHING differently. I also understand that I cannot communicate with her as I would another man. I understand that when she speaks, I often take what she says wrong. In other words, sometimes she doesn't say what I think she says. Confused? Well, keep reading.

Men are, for the most part, cognitive in their communication and approach to life. Cognitive generally means that everything in life is pretty much black and white. We speak mostly to provide information for the purpose of fixing things. Facts are honored. Limits and boundaries are enforced. And, we men are very good at doing these things because we usually center on one issue, deal with it, put it aside, and go on with our lives. If we don't see a problem, it doesn't exist, whether we resolved it or not. This is why it is so important to resolve problems before going to bed at night. A man can fight and quarrel with his wife, say all kinds of evil things, and then give up and go to bed without resolving anything. The next morning he awakens refreshed. His wife is a bit more pleasant than she was the night before. So, to him, there is no longer a problem. He goes on living in his fantasy "there-are-no-problems-in-my-life" world.

This is why there is a biblical directive to deal with your problems before you go to bed. "Be angry and do not sin, and do not let the sun go down on your wrath" *(Ephesians 4:26)*. This directive was not designed to keep you from getting a good night's sleep. It was designed to keep you from messing up a hundred tomorrows by resolving the problem today.

Women are, for the most part, affective in their communication and approach to life. Affective generally means that everything in life is intertwined. Women speak with the desire to create an emotional attachment. Feelings are honored. Limits and boundaries should be talked about and remodeled according to each situation. Women think more in concepts rather than single factoids. They are able to think about, and talk about, more than one issue at a time. If a problem is set aside or ignored, it still exists, and the feelings surrounding the problem continue to increase. So, the couple goes to bed after fighting and quarreling. She gets up and the problem is still real. She deals with the problem alone because the husband is living in la-la land. She won't speak about the problem again until the pain becomes too unbearable. So, one week, two weeks, one month, or six months later she will open up and vent about that horrible night. The husband is shocked: "How can that still be a problem when it happened so long ago?" The wife is shocked: "How can you say that this isn't a problem when we never resolved it?" So they have another fight about the same issue and go to bed, again, without resolving it.

Who's wrong here? Both! The husband's need is to fix and forget, something his wife is not allowing to happen. The wife's need is to connect with her husband so she knows that he feels what she feels, something her husband is not allowing to happen. So they limp off into the future still not understanding.

The popular book, *Men are from Mars, Women are from Venus* (John Gray, HarperCollins Publishers, 1992), vividly illustrates the differences in the way men and women view life. In fact, it's kind of corny. Aren't Mars and Venus like a million miles away from each other? Yes, and that's how far apart husbands and wives are at times when it comes to conflict. Remember, understanding is half the battle.

Men and women are different when it comes to pain. So, I'm out in my garage, hammering away at a small project, when I hit my thumb with a hammer. I yell and scream, jump up and down, suck on my thumb, and offer a few words that you're not supposed to say in polite company. My wife hears the ruckus. She comes to the garage and lovingly asks, "What's wrong?" What do men usually say here? "Nothing!" I'm processing my pain the way I know how. I just want the pain over with. But my wife wants to connect with me, to share my pain and strengthen our marriage. I just pushed her away and refused her that opportunity to connect. Understanding is half the battle.

Men and women are different when it comes to intimacy and sex. I got married when I was 19, at the peak of my sexual eagerness (horny-ness). I believed that I would marry and have sex every night for the rest of my life. Isn't that what all married couples do? Well, I found out quickly that this would not be the case. But I didn't understand. So I used my cognitive skills to promote more sex. When my wife wasn't feeling good, I thought: "My wife doesn't feel good—sex makes you feel good—let's have sex—then she'll feel good!" It sounded good and logical to me. But not to her. Understanding will avert these kinds of problems.

#2- IN A HEALTHY MARRIAGE, CONFLICT IS NOT A FOUR-LETTER WORD.

Here's how husbands and wives become bitter enemies. Some conflict arises. The husband processes the information in his cognitive way, discovers a solution, loves his wife enough to fix the problem, and tries to share the information. The wife processes the information in her affective way, discovers the hurtful emotions that surround the problem, loves her husband enough to try to connect with him to make the marriage better, and attempts to share the information. He doesn't understand her, she doesn't understand him, so they go off to the separate corners. Conflict now becomes a source of conflict. In other words, just the idea of conflict turns negative. He says: "There she goes again. I can't do anything right. I'm in trouble all the time." She says the same things.

Conflict is not a bad thing. It should be viewed as an opportunity to change something for the better. Marriage is a living, growing relationship. Think of it like buying a pair of jeans. A young boy enters his first year at the local high school. He dresses in his favorite jeans for that first day of classes. But the jeans are tight, it hurts to button and zip. The legs of the jeans are so short that hairy leg is showing between the bottom of the jeans and the top of the sock. He comes to you complaining that his pants don't fit any more. So, what are you going to say? "Those jeans were just fine when we bought them three years ago. Quit complaining and get to school!" How ridiculous is it to make a teen wear the same clothes that fit him three years and fifty pounds ago? The pain of tight pants and the whining of a young teen signal a need for change. So, change for the better.

Conflict may be a signal that one partner doesn't feel the same appreciation he/she once felt. We begin marriage with romance and anticipation that romance will always be there. But we find ourselves getting into the humdrum routines of life. We work, eat, sleep, then get up the next day to do the same thing. Conflict, ill feelings, may be simply a signal to both of you that you need to rekindle the romance in your marriage. So, change for the better.

Conflict should never be avoided or ignored. Think about this: every conflict that you have had in your marriage that has not been completely resolved is still with you. They just float up into a cloud that hangs over your marriage. Now, whenever new, small problems arise, the weight of all past unresolved problems may come crashing down.

So, I throw my dirty socks at the hamper and one of them falls on the floor. I walk away. My wife says, "Hey, pick up your sock!" Well, why is she talking to me like that? I respond, "You pick it up!" She's ticked. She says, "It's your sock!" I respond, "You're closer!" After a few more rounds of accusations, I say something incredibly stupid like, "Well, it's woman's work anyway!" She stomps off and slams one door. I go off and slam another door. We don't talk to each other for three days. Is our marriage on the brink of destruction because of one silly sock on the floor? Well, yes. But you're not just arguing over the sock on the floor. You're arguing over every problem you've ever had that has not been resolved. We must resolve each problem as soon as it happens, for the sake of our marriage. For the sake of our future. In a healthy marriage, the couple realizes how much better off they will be after the conflict is resolved.

#3- In a healthy marriage, partners give RESPECT and HONOR.

In all my years of counseling and helping married couples, I am amazed, but not surprised any more, when couples come in and say the nastiest things about each other. I have heard the worst names and most horrible descriptions of people that were once lifted up as "the love of my life." This behavior is a symptom of a couple that has lost its ability to communicate. Without communication there is no intimacy, closeness. So the opposite happens. Every day in every way they drift further and further apart. Anger replaces patience and hate replaces love. This will never help.

Dr. Bob Truism #4:

RESPECT is how you treat each other in private. HONOR is how you treat each other in public.

In healthy marriages, couples have learned that no matter what conflict is occurring or what emotions are being felt, respect and honor must continue. Respect and honor do not mean that you ignore conflict or avoid confrontation when they are necessary. But these attitudes must be present so the heart is not damaged while working out the conflicts.

There are many ideas on what respect and honor look like in marriage. But according to Dr. Bob, that's me, RESPECT is how you treat each other in private, HONOR is how you treat each other in public.

Let's start with respect. In my marriage, my wife occupies a place of respect in my life and in my heart. So, in every situation, even those situations in which I disagree with her, I still must respect her as Queen of My Heart. What does this look like? Think about our last presidential election. The man I did not vote for was elected. I have problems with that. However, if he were to come into my office I would immediately stand. I would call him "Sir." I might even ask if I could have a picture taken with him, after all, he is the most famous and most powerful man in the world. But given the opportunity to discuss issues with him, I would not be shy to tell him where I disagree with him and why. But the whole time I would use respectful words and gestures.

In marriage, husbands should look at their wives as if they were royalty, as some famous and powerful person that stands in your presence. Now, don't avoid confrontation when necessary, but use words and behavior that prove you believe he/she is royalty. So, which quote best describes how you should treat your husband/wife in conflict?

"Why do you have to be so stupid? EVERY TIME I come home you have something new to gripe about. Complete strangers are nicer to me than you. I should have stayed at work!"

Or ...

"Honey, I'm having a problem with how we talked this afternoon. Do you think we could sit down and talk about this? I'll be ready whenever you are."

Do you see the difference? Don't avoid the confrontation. But handle it respectfully.

Now, let's talk about honor. So you go to the office or workplace and hear people talking negatively about their mates. You can (1) join in and berate your spouse to fit in with your friends (he/she will never know), or you can (2) tell your friends how wonderful your spouse is. Choice #1 is always wrong. Too many people are degrading marriage when they degrade their spouses. And, if you hang around people who are negative about marriage, you will become negative as well. Then you will bring that negativity home and mess everything up there.

To dishonor your mate is what I call hydraulic behavior. You know, hydraulics? The system your mechanic uses to put your car up in the air so he can change your oil? Well what happens is that somewhere in the garage there are pipes full of oil that are connected to the mechanism that will lift your car. The oil in the pipes on one side of the garage is pushed down which causes the car on the other side of the garage to rise. That's about the extent of my knowledge of hydraulic lifts. But in life we see people often using this theory, believing that if I criticize or put down someone else it will make me look better. First graders do it, too. It's not pretty. But husbands and wives fall into this trap all the time. They put down the person who gives them the most grief in order to feel good, as least for a moment or two. Don't fall into this trap.

Here's what you should do. Everyone else is saying bad things, but you say, "I'm sorry your wives are so awful. My wife is wonderful." Then go home and tell your wife what you did. I guarantee you will get a kiss out of it. Wives, do the same thing. While the other women are complaining about their husbands, say, "I'm sorry your husbands are so creepy. Mine is fantastic!" Then go home and tell your husband what you did. I guarantee you will get a kiss. Well, he'll probably want more than that.

Now, don't lie. Don't say that your husband brought you breakfast in bed or that your wife rubbed your feet if those things did not happen. But find something about your mate that is wonderful and beautiful and brag about them in public. You'll be glad you did.

#4- IN A HEALTHY MARRIAGE, COUPLES HAVE THE SAME HOPES AND DREAMS.

When you got married you volunteered to give up selfish hopes and dreams and volunteered to discover hopes and dreams that you both can share. Now, don't get me wrong, this does not mean that you abandon all your plans that you made before marriage. But if you keep them make sure that your mate is an integral part of the plan.

Hopes, dreams, and goals should be talked about before the couple marries. But if this did not happen, there is no time like the present. In fact, every couple ought to sit down once a year and talk about these things. What do you want your marriage to look like one, five, and ten years from now? What about real estate and investments? What about financial freedom? What about education for you or the children? Vacations, safaris, once-in-a-lifetime trips? Grow closer together as a couple as you plan your future, together.

#5- IN A HEALTHY MARRIAGE, COUPLES HAVE A SPIRITUAL OUTLOOK.

To cement a healthy marriage, many couples share a spiritual outlook on life. In other words, they believe that life can be more than just a 9 to 5 job. They can affect more than just themselves and their families. So, they involve themselves in spiritual ventures—things that are bigger than themselves. It elevates them from the mundane to an almost supernatural plane. And, if a couple can do this together, the marriage enters new and exciting heights.

And it's healthy, too.

Carl Jung, famous psychologist of the 1940s and 1950s, said, "Of all of my clients in the second half of life, most of their neuroses would disappear if they would have a spiritual outlook on life."

So, go beyond yourselves with benevolence, humanitarian ventures, or altruistic ventures. All of those fancy words mean that you look beyond your own home and family and find others that you can help. Buy a gift for someone. Take a meal to an older couple down the street. Go to the soup kitchens around the holidays and serve meals to the homeless. Do for others without expecting anything in return. And, remember the Mother Teresa Effect? You'll be happier and healthier, and so will your children.

Go beyond yourselves with adventure. As a couple you need to plan some adventure you can do as a couple that not only will provide you with fantastic memories and stories to share, but will bring you closer since you did it together. Go on a cruise. Go on a safari in Africa. Visit England or France or some other foreign place you've wanted to see. Decide on some fantastic voyage you can share. If you have no money, make a plan to do something special five years from now. Start saving. Then go and have a blast.

Go beyond yourselves with religion. Most religions

have as a basic tenet the idea of serving your fellow man or being a blessing to your community. This is definitely a way to go beyond yourselves, especially in you believe in a Higher Power that you would like to honor. But remember, the more you serve God or your fellow man, the happier and healthier you will be.

#6- In a healthy marriage, couples wear blinders.

We live in a sensual world. Sexuality is presented in positive and negative lights. Advertisers use sensuality to engage your senses in order to tempt you into purchasing their products. Because of all this, we have opened our minds to "what if" or "what's so wrong about that" when it comes to cheating or fantasizing. Oooo, we'd better be careful.

As a married man or a married woman, you must wear blinders. Here's Dr. Bob's definition of blinders—an implement that keeps out of your eyes the things that don't belong in your eyes. If we don't make a conscious effort to focus only on our mates when it comes to love and sexuality, we can easily be tempted to fantasize or cheat, both of which will damage or destroy your marriage.

Almost anything in life can be designed to attract us. Take, for example, pure beauty. Who gets to decide what pure beauty is? Advertisers paint pictures of pure beauty to make you believe that their standard is the standard of beauty. If your wife wears the right bra she will look like a model. If your husband buys that complete gym package he will have six-pack abs like the guy in the commercial. They are promoting the idea that happiness is found when you look like them. Don't let them suck you into a false view of beauty.

Pure beauty is whatever you want it to be. That's one of the benefits or blessings the Creator gave to us. We can decide who or what is beautiful. If I decide that my wife is the most beautiful woman in my life, she becomes the most beautiful. If I decide that she is ugly, she becomes uglier every day. It's my choice. The point here is, if you wear blinders, you focus on your mate, and he/she becomes more beautiful every day.

Comparisons are a sure way to destroy your marriage. The minute you compare your mate to any other person, your mate always loses! So I get up early like I always do, have some coffee, read the paper and prepare to go off to work. My wife rolls out of bed, puts on that robe that I hate, her hair is mashed to one side, and her breath smells like dragon's feet. We have a little argument that ends with, "Fine, just go to work!" to which I reply, "Fine, I'm going to work!" So, I get to my office and my secretary is already there. She is pleasantly dressed, hair beautifully combed, and she greets me with respect, "Good morning,

Dr. Whiddon, how are you today?" So I look at her, and then remember the thing I left at home … See how easy it would be to start focusing on another woman?

Unresolved conflicts can push us towards some other person and destroy our marriage. When conflicts pile up in the cloud that hangs over us, it seems like our mates NEVER understand or NEVER have the time to truly listen to our complaints. But that person at work, the one with whom you have no history, seems willing to take the time not only to listen to you but to empathize with your feelings. Once again, your mate loses in this kind of comparison.

The lure of freedom might attract us to someone else. Here's what happens. A man decides that his wife is the total problem in his marriage. "If I could just get out of this marriage I can find someone much better." So, he divorces his wife (50 percent of all first marriages end in divorce), and he finds another woman to marry (usually the next spouse is a lot like the first one). Soon into the second marriage he notices that this new wife has the same problems that his first wife had. "How can I be so unlucky as to find two horrible women to marry?" With less patience, he divorces this wife quicker (75 percent of all second marriages end in divorce). This man thought freedom from his first wife would solve all his problems. But he failed to understand that HE was at least 50 percent of the problems in his first marriage. Freedom does not resolve your problems.

You must stay in your marriage and work things out. I'll show you how. Keep reading. But don't look to someone else for happiness. Wear blinders! Get to work on your own marriage. You will be happier and healthier. I guarantee it.

#7- IN A HEALTHY MARRIAGE, COUPLES CELEBRATE MARRIAGE WITH INTIMACY.

There is a difference between sex and intimacy. Sex is the physical act designed to bring one or both to climax. Intimacy is the atmosphere of closeness and connection in which sex occurs. More about this in the next chapter. But keep in mind that in a healthy marriage, sex comes naturally as a celebration of a close, intimate relationship. So, when things go wrong in the bedroom, don't work on sex, work on intimacy. Build your intimacy, or closeness, or connection. Then, sex should come naturally.

#8- IN A HEALTHY MARRIAGE, COUPLES SERVE ONE ANOTHER.

The single greatest attitude that underlies almost every problem in marriage is selfishness. We were born into this world selfish, demanding attention in every aspect of life.

But then we were trained, or at least our parents tried to train us, in helping others, being kind to others, letting others go first, etc. In marriage, when conflict arises and goes unresolved, many of us revert to the former behavior to cope. This doesn't work. It only makes things worse. The opposite of selfishness is being of service to each other. This is one of the healthiest behaviors in marriage.

In healthy marriages, the couple understands the unique relationship between service and happiness. We've already shared with you the Mother Teresa Effect. Medical science has supported the idea that health and self esteem are natural byproducts of serving others. So, do this in marriage.

As a healthy couple, find ways to serve one another in every aspect of life:

- In everyday life—couples find ways to serve through encouraging words ("I'm proud of you," "You're wonderful," "You're beautiful") or through performing acts of kindness (doing each other's chores, foot rubs, back rubs, loving gifts).
- In the business world—sending encouraging messages through the phone, email, text messages, hidden notes in briefcases and purses, listening to one another as you unwind from the hectic workday.
- In conflict—even when it comes to conflict

resolution, there should be a "service" component since all conflict begins with selfishness.

- In the bedroom—when it comes to intimacy and sex, my attitude should always be, "what can I give" rather than "what can I get." Try it this way. Your sex life will improve dramatically.

One more thing about service or servanthood— serving is enjoyable because you think of the other person more than yourself. But beware, if you expect something in return, you will revert to a selfish attitude even when you are doing acts of kindness. This will hurt you!

I remember watching a promo for the Dr. Phil show. There was an attractive woman sitting on stage beside her quadriplegic husband who sat in his wheelchair. She was telling the story of how they had a Cinderella-like marriage for eight years. Money was good, sex was fantastic, and their future looked bright. But the husband got into an accident and lost the use of his arms and legs. They had been married for eleven years when they came on the Dr. Phil show. She explained how she had done nothing but serve her husband for the past three years. She's tired. She said things like, "I think it's time for me. It's time for me to be happy." Now, I understand Dr. Phil does not stay silent often, but he was quiet, letting this woman keep talking, giving her enough rope to hang herself with. Finally, Dr.

Phil opened his mouth and said, "SELFISH is not a big enough word to describe you."

The woman was serving, but she was miserable. Why? Because she kept thinking about herself more than her husband. WHENEVER you think more about yourself than someone else, you will ALWAYS be miserable.

Healthy married couples serve one another and perform acts of kindness without expecting anything in return. As a result, they themselves are happier and healthier. But another amazing thing happens—the one being served is happier and healthier and more willing to serve as well. It's a win/win situation!

The Design and Placement of Intimacy in Marriage

KNOWLEDGE IS THE KEY! We need to understand intimacy. It's not that hard of a concept. But many people mix up intimacy with sex. They go together. But they're different. Understanding where intimacy fits in with your marriage will help you have a better marriage and a better sex life.

Men like sex—a lot! Women like intimacy—a lot! But men think intimacy is sex and mess it up all the time. Because of this, men are always searching for signs, signals that their wives might be approachable for sex at a certain time. We try to find shortcuts so we don't have to work so hard at getting to the good stuff. Men, STOP searching for signs and signals. You'll probably miss them anyway.

I remember, as a young minister, one Sunday morning I got up early like I usually did to get ready for the day ahead. I was in the shower, leaning over to rinse the shampoo out of my hair, when I noticed that someone had gotten into the shower with me. After I rinsed the shampoo and wiped my eyes, I turned around and noticed that it was my wife, with a big smile on her face. I thought, "Hmm, this is going to be a great day." So we kissed a little and washed each other's backs. After we showered I toweled her off and she toweled me off. She wrapped her towel around her, gave me a wink, and went off to the bedroom. I thought, "Hmm, my wife is in a great mood this morning." So I ... stayed in the bathroom for a while, you know, combing my hair, shaving, trimming my nose hair, all the things I needed to do to be ready for church.

After a while I went to the bedroom to get dressed. My wife was in the master bathroom at the time. And, I noticed the bed wasn't made, which was weird since she usually makes the bed as soon as our feet hit the floor. So I thought, "Hmm ..." and I began to make the bed for her. After all, she was in such a good mood, I just wanted to do something for her. As I was making up the bed, I noticed that small candles on our massive headboard were all lit. I thought, "Hmm ..." and I kept on making up the bed. Then I noticed that the stereo on our headboard was on, playing soft, romantic music. So, I thought, "Hmm ..." and I kept on making the bed. Then I got dressed and went out to the living room to read the paper before church, thinking "what a wonderful day this is, my wife is in such a good mood."

About a half hour later my wife came out of the bedroom, and she was mad! She stomped around the house, slamming cabinet doors and silverware drawers. And I thought, "What's this? We were having such a good morning. What could have gone wrong?" She puttered around some more, not saying anything to me. We got the kids up and got them dressed and fed. And about 20 minutes before we had to leave for church, I thought, "We've got to get this cleared up. We can't go to church mad." So I got in her face and said, "Honey, I thought we were having such a great morning. What happened?"

She looked me in the eyes, she grabbed the lapels of my suit jacket, and said, "Look! When your naked wife gets in the shower with you it ALWAYS means she wants to have sex with you." So I thought, "Hmm ... Hey! There's the signal!" And then I said, "We've got 20 minutes. Let's go!" But she didn't want to. She wasn't in the mood.

Signals? Ha! I use this story in my workshops and it gets a big laugh. But most men can relate to missing signals that weren't nearly as clear as the ones I had. The problem with looking for signs and signals is that we are trying to bypass our need to grow the intimacy in our marriage.

There was a study released in 2007 that attempted to discover the true stimuli that bring men and women to the point of sexual desire. I found it in my local newspaper. ("The Anatomy of Desire" *Oregonian*, April 11, 2007.)

The study, that included researchers from the University of Utah, the Center for Addiction and Mental Health in Toronto, and the University of Amsterdam, set out to find what triggered our desire for sex. They found that men were easily stimulated and needed little help. But for women, here's what they found:

> ... 93 percent to 96 percent of the 655 respondents strongly endorsed statements that linked sexual arousal to "feeling connected to" or "loved by" a partner, and to the belief that the partner is "really interested in me as a person."

The researchers concluded that there were no shortcuts for women. What women needed was intimacy. They needed to feel connected to their partners before they could become involved in sexual activity.

So, intimacy is what women need. But let's not put the entire responsibility on them. Men need intimacy, too. They just don't know it. However, if men got their way all the time, sex would become boring. Maybe it has already become boring in your marriage.

A marriage or relationship centered around sex usually only lasts a year or so. Look at any Hollywood marriage that puts a hunky leading man with a beautiful lingerie model. We are no longer surprised when they end it all so quickly after it starts. Guys are thinking, "Is he crazy? He wants to dump her?" Of course they are viewing this problem from the sex viewpoint, what sex must be like with such a gorgeous woman. The women are thinking, "Is she crazy? She wants to dump him?" Of course they are viewing this problem from the same viewpoint of what sex, but also romance, must be like with such a gorgeous man. But the celebrity couple splits anyway. The reason: sex without a growing intimate relationship gets very boring.

So, let's talk intimacy. Here are the basics:

- Intimacy is the atmosphere in which sex occurs.
- Sex is the physical act that includes foreplay, intercourse, and afterglow, designed to bring one or both to climax
- Intimacy is the atmosphere in which couples realize an emotional or spiritual connection
- Intimacy does not necessarily include sex hugging, touching, kissing, cuddling for emotional connection
- Sex is designed to take place within a committed intimate relationship
- Intimacy is not designed to prohibit sex—intimate married partners celebrate intimacy with sex
- Intimacy is a lifestyle

See the difference? It'll get clearer as we go along.

Intimacy is a matter of survival! Sex is not a life-or-death matter. And, no, a boy won't explode if he doesn't get sex. But a man does need intimacy, or he might die!

When we are born into this world, we are born to two loving parents that think we are the cutest things to ever grace this earth. They hold us, kiss us, and blabber to us in some "goo-goo ga-ga" infantile chatter that even we don't understand. But it gets us to smile. POW! We are in an intimate relationship. Remember, intimacy is the atmosphere of closeness or connectedness. We immediately connect to our parents. The father shows us the masculine side of life, the tough, cognitive outlook on life. The mother shows us the softer side of life, the gentle, affective outlook on life. And, if we didn't have this intimate relationship with our parents, we would die.

In world history, Fredrick II, the Emperor over Germany and other neighboring nations in the early 1200s (also called the Holy Roman Emperor) decided that he needed to know what language babies would speak if they never heard their parents speak. It is claimed he was seeking to discover what language would have been given to Adam and Eve. Fredrick's historian wrote that he commanded

"foster-mothers and nurses to suckle and bathe and wash the children, but in no ways to prattle or speak with them; for he would have learnt whether

they would speak the Hebrew language (which had been the first), or Greek, or Latin, or Arabic, or perchance the tongue of their parents of whom they had been born. But he laboured in vain, for the children could not live without clappings of the hands, and gestures, and gladness of countenance, and blandishments."

Fredrick II never found out what language babies would speak if they were not influenced by parents. The reason for the failed experiment? All of the infants died. Today we know what killed the babies. It was a medical problem. It's called "failure to thrive." If a baby is not held, kissed, and talked to in goo-goo-esque language, they will not thrive. Intimacy IS a matter of survival.

A boy needs his mom and his dad the whole time he is growing up. A girl needs her mom and dad the whole time she is growing up. But at a certain time in life, the boy and girl having needs and desires that parents cannot fulfill, choose to leave the intimate atmosphere of life at home, join with someone of the opposite sex, and begin a new intimate relationship. Together they face the world. They are a couple that will influence mankind by being a benefit to society. Intimacy keeps going and keeps growing. It's the circle of life.

Sex also enters this new marriage. It begins as a celebration of the committed relationship. And it's beautiful and wonderful and happens a lot! And the couple just keeps getting closer and closer. It's great to be a newlywed!

The physiology of intimacy and sex. To further de-fog marriage, we must understand what happens to us during sex. Not just the ecstasy of orgasm, but the spiritual and emotional connection that couples experience. Here's how I explain it in counseling and in our marriage workshops.

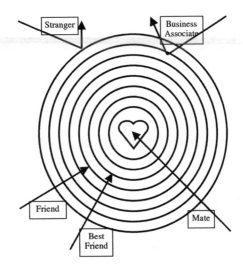

The heart in this picture is the tenderest part of your heart. It's where sex happens. Sex happens there because of the emotional excitement of two beings getting as close to one another as humanly possible.

The rings around the heart are the self-imposed protective barriers that guard that most tender part. You decide how close each person gets to you. So, you get a call, at dinnertime, from a guy that butchers your last name, and talks to you as if he is a long lost friend: "Hi, Mr. Smith! How are you today?" It's a salesman. He's trying to sell you something, even though they almost always say, "I'm not trying to sell you anything." What do you do? Do you feel sorry for this intruder and try to let him down politely? Do you make up some excuse about having his product already? Do you open up and tell some truths about being out of work or that the bills are running amok? No! You simply say, "I'm not interested" and hang up. It's not a lie. You don't have to engage this interrupter in polite conversation. He's a salesman who has rudely interrupted your dinner. Hang up! That's what the barriers are for. You would never allow a stranger that close into your life.

A business associate is a little different. You have forged a relationship and you may feel comfortable revealing a little bit more about yourself. You might talk about your kids, birthdays, likes and dislikes. But that's all.

A friend you would let closer into your heart. You might share hopes and dreams, struggles and successes. A best friend would be allowed closer into your heart. Your deep secrets might be shared. You may laugh and cry with this person because you feel so comfortable.

But when you marry, you voluntarily open up all the barriers to the tenderest part of your heart. Why? Because the intimacy has grown. You feel comfortable. You allow yourself to be vulnerable. There are no more secrets. There is nothing else hidden. Your life, your self, your everything is laid completely open to your mate. Then sex happens. And it's beautiful.

Now, mull these questions over in your mind.

#1—If this chart is true, then why wait until marriage to engage in sexual activities? Could it be that sex, because it allows someone into the tenderest part of you, should happen only when trust is built? And how is trust built? By talking, communicating, hoping, and dreaming. These are descriptions of intimacy.

#2—If this chart is true, then why allow someone SLOWLY into your heart? Could it have something to do with the building of trust? How is trust built? You need time to learn about the other person. You need time to become comfortable in everything about him/her. The most important thing in marriage is not sex! The most important thing in marriage is intimacy. Take time to build up this intimacy (engagement, courtship) so you can freely open all the barriers.

#3—If this chart is true, what should you be able to enjoy before, during, and after intercourse? Security! You need to be confident that what you and your mate share will not be shared with anyone else, whether physically (the affair) or vocally (sharing your secrets with others).

Short-circuiting intimacy and sex. The previous chart showed the ideal situation of a couple waiting until marriage to engage in sex. But we know that most people don't wait. In fact, it is estimated that, in general, 85 to 90 percent of all couples have sex before they are married. This statistic is shockingly true even among religious people who have a "divine calling" to stay pure until marriage. Why is this? Because most people have a fogged-up idea that sex is proof of love. Instead of pursuing intimacy, confidence, trust and security, people force their way into another's heart to get sex. This just brings on a whole new set of problems, problems that will affect future relationships.

The following chart illustrates an assault on one's heart. Instead of allowing a person to build up a commitment and voluntarily open up all the barriers, someone has forced his/her way into the tenderest part of the heart. Assault, of course, includes all the illegal activity of sexual criminals in our society—the rapist, the child molester. Remember, sex outside of a committed relationship gets boring. So the criminal, to continue to be satisfied in his evil pursuits,

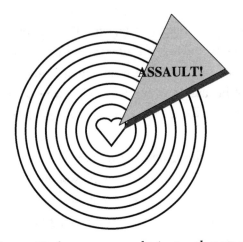

must of necessity become more deviant and more violent. Assault also includes the young man who pressures his girlfriend into having sex. When he becomes successful at this, he has taught himself "Well, that's the way girls are. I have to trick them or force them into sex." He'll take this attitude later into marriage and treat his wife the same way. For the young woman who gives in after trying to fight off the persistent boyfriend, she will start to believe "Well, that's the way boys are. They have to trick me and force themselves on me." She will take this attitude later into marriage and perhaps become fearful of sex, waiting until her husband forces himself on her.

Sex should be a beautiful thing. It should be enjoyable and fulfilling. It should be a celebration of a growing, intimate relationship. Never try to bypass the one thing that makes sex so good—intimacy!

So, where can I get me some intimacy? Here are some ways you and your mate can strengthen your intimacy:

- Have deep conversations. Women make connections through communication.
- Resolve conflicts as soon as they appear. Ill feelings or grudges hinder intimacy.
- Treat each other like royalty. Even when disagreeing, be respectful of how you speak and how you act.
- Share in each other's hobbies and activities.
- Dream with each other. Make plans for a once-in-a-lifetime cruise or safari.
- Touch and cuddle.

There is a special way to grow intimacy. But first you have to take the sex/intimacy quiz.

Intimacy Quiz:

How long does it take for a man to prepare for intercourse?

How long does it take for woman to prepare for intercourse?

How long after sex does it take for a man to become temporarily uninterested in intimacy?

How long after sex does it take for a woman to become temporarily uninterested in intimacy?

Well, for question #1, I've heard anywhere from 5 to 30 seconds. But if your answer falls between those two numbers, you are way off. A man is almost always ready for sex. The woman is a more complicated person. For question #2, it may take anywhere from 30 minutes to several hours for her to be in the mood for intercourse. Men are like microwaves, ready and fast. Women are like crock pots, taking a while to warm up and get the job done. Or maybe men are like DSL, always on, while women are like a dial-up internet connection. Takes a long time.

For question #3, men become disinterested, temporarily, almost immediately after orgasm. They even secrete an enzyme in their brains that causes them to want to sleep. So, falling asleep after intercourse is normal and natural. But for question #4, women take a lot longer to become disinterested in sex. Look at this chart. Women take longer

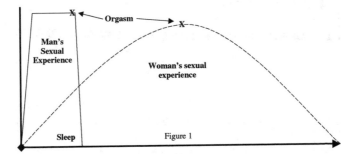

Figure 1

to get to the point of orgasm, then take a while to come down from the emotional high they experience in a full intimate/sexual/orgasmic connection with their mate.

What would happen if (as in Figure 1) the man jumps into sex, has an orgasm, then quits before his wife is even halfway to the point of orgasm herself? How about frustration, disappointment, unhappiness, and rejection. Is this the way you want your wife to feel during sex?

Now look at the next chart. Let's say the man does take better care of his wife as she grows towards orgasm. And maybe if it is not a simultaneous orgasm (which is quite difficult for some) they climax close to the same time. But,

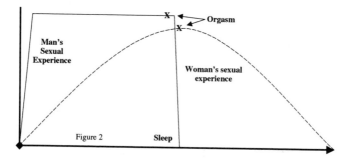

if the man falls asleep at that point, what happens to the wife? She is still coming down from the high. She wants to cuddle. She wants to enjoy the closeness. She wants to feel his hand gently stroking her cheek and forehead. Guys, this is the perfect time to grow intimacy in your marriage. If you fight the urge to roll over and sleep, you can help intimacy become stronger after sex than it was before sex.

And what a blessing for the next time you approach her for intercourse.

Hopefully, intimacy and sex are becoming clearer to you. The fog is lifting and you can see the possibilities of having great intimacy and a great sex life. Here are some final thoughts:

- **Sex begins in the kitchen.** Not that you have sex in the kitchen … unless you want to have sex in the kitchen. But this means that creating an atmosphere of intimacy is an all-day affair. In fact, it is a lifestyle that must be adopted. Don't just be amorous when you want sex. Build intimacy every waking moment.

- **Don't look at your mate as a sex object, but rather as a life partner.** The religious people may object, "But we're married now. I can lust after my wife, right?" Well, yes and no. Now that you're married, lust is not forbidden. But whenever you do lust and pursue lust, you have turned your mate into an object to play with. This is never good.

- **Spend a lot of time talking about intimacy.** Couples should have deep conversations often. You ought to talk about this once a month or so. Talk about your likes and dislikes, what might be missing in your relationship.

- **Spend a lot of time encouraging and building**

each other up. This goes a long way in building intimacy, closeness.

- **If you are ever frustrated about your sex-life, don't work on sex, work on intimacy.** Sex should be a natural celebration of a strong intimate relationship.

There is an old saying, or maybe I just made it up, that goes like this: *Intimacy is like a cake, and sex is like the icing on the cake.* If this is true, then what flavor of icing should you put on your cake? Chocolate? Whipped cream? Strawberry? Well, here's the correct answer:

Any kind you like, as long as it is pleasurable for both!

There are no rules, anywhere, about what a couple can or cannot do in the bedroom (unless it crosses into illegal activity). As a married couple you are free to do whatever you want. But it should be guided by this mantra. If it is not pleasurable to your mate, don't do it, don't try it, don't talk about it. Even in intimacy and sex, you are in it as a servant. "What can I do for my mate to make him/her happy?"

Next to financial matters, sex is the most argued and fought about topic in marriage. Understanding where intimacy and sex are designed to fit into marriage will make half of your problems go away. The fog is about to lift.

The Seven Natural Stages of Marriage

KNOWLEDGE IS THE KEY! Marriage is a living, changing, growing organism. It is a living, changing, growing relationship. All marriages, in general, go through the same ups and downs. Understanding these natural stages will help prepare you for when change occurs and will give you the knowledge of necessary changes to make your marriage stronger today than it was yesterday.

Stage One—Pure Love! This covers the time right before we marry and right after the wedding. When we fall in love, we enter the first stage of marriage. Even though couples are not usually married 10 minutes after meeting each other, they still enter into a relationship that will naturally lead to marriage. They may not make it all the way to the altar. But consider this: very few marriages begin without some time devoted to romance and courtship. This is the stage of pure love.

Now, I'm going to give you the true definition of love. Memorize it! You'll thank me forever! Here again is the technical definition of Pure Love:

Doing Stuff for One Another

Here's what happened. When you first fell in love, you naturally secreted chemicals into your brain that caused an endorphin-like effect. It was euphoria! You were high—in love. Or at least, that's how it felt. But the feeling wasn't love at all. The important thing to notice is what the feeling caused you to do. You began doing stuff for the one with whom you were in love. You know, the gifts, the poems, the walking hand in hand in the moonlight. The doing stuff was love. Love means you consider the other person so valuable that you are willing to DO anything for him/her. But then, when you did something out of the ordinary, out of the blue, not expecting anything in return, you experienced another sensation—"satisfaction euphoria" because you made another person happy. This sensation is the natural result of the servant attitude. So here's what really happens: You "fall in love" or get high over this person you have chosen. You practice the true meaning of love by "doing stuff for each other." Then you experience

Dr. Bob Truism #5:

Love means I consider you so VALUABLE that I am willing to do anything for you!

the natural satisfaction built in to every act of love.

Do you remember when you fell in love, and all the excitement of sharing and caring for each other? Some will say, "Yeah! That's what I want. I want that feeling of falling in love again. I want that excitement back." Well, you can't. The chemical invasion of your brain that happens at the moment you fall in love was designed to jump-start your marriage. The chemicals, the high, make you want to do things for the other person. And since the high usually lasts from 18 months to three years, you have plenty of time to make these acts of service habits that will last a lifetime. Your relationship goes deeper and deeper into intimacy and connectedness. And, what's supposed to happen, when that high wears off, is that you will continue to do acts of service because of the close, intimate relationship you have developed and because of the satisfaction you feel afterwards. And you will go deeper and deeper into your loving relationship.

Dr. James Dobson, noted psychologist, told a group of teenagers in his video series *The Myth of Safe Sex,* "Everything in the male/female relationship is designed to lead to intercourse." Think about it. This is absolutely true.

Do you remember the ecstatic feeling you got when you first met that special someone? It was great. But after a while, just meeting him/her wasn't as satisfying. So you went deeper. Remember the first time you held hands with someone of the opposite sex? Wasn't it great? But after a while it wasn't as satisfying. So you went deeper, arms around the shoulders, arms around the hips.

Do you remember the excitement of your first kiss? Did you practice on the mirror like I did? I remember there was a girl in my church who was three years older than me, and we made an appointment to meet after church, in the basement of the church building, and kiss. Well, I didn't want her to think I was a complete moron, so I went home and practiced kissing. That night I could hardly concentrate on anything that was going on. When church was over I went downstairs for the prearranged, first ever kiss. I remember we didn't talk much but went right to the kiss. It was good…but some of her spit got into my mouth. It made me sick! Ick! I thought I was going to throw up. But…I soon got over it. Kissing became natural and very pleasurable. But after a while, even the kissing wasn't as satisfying and pleasurable as it was at first.

You see how all this works? That's why we need to warn our teens about this natural phenomenon so they don't go too far outside a committed marriage. Adults, we need to be careful as well. Most affairs are with someone from the workplace. We innocently flirt with someone of the opposite sex one day. It's cool. It's pleasurable. But the next time it's not as pleasurable, so you must go deeper. That's how we're designed. Be careful.

Back to stage one. Pure love is when we do stuff for each other. It's a great time of life. But remember, the feeling isn't love. The doing is love!

Stage Two—Celebration. This stage covers the first two years of marriage. Everything about this stage is a celebration. It begins with that romantic wedding that was dreamed of and planned for months. The family was there. Friends were there. It was festive. It was glamorous. It was a celebration.

The honeymoon is a celebration. The newlywed couple goes off to exciting places, or not so faraway places, to celebrate their union. The sex is a celebration of love. The companionship is a celebration of love. The adventure is a celebration of love. Well, you get it. The new couple celebrates all over the place.

The first apartment or home is a celebration. Many of the women will change their names and take on the husband's name. Celebration!

Here's what all this celebration does for the couple:

- **It further cements the relationship.** The wedding joins them, but the going off together alone makes the union even stronger.
- **It makes serving easy and pleasurable.** The couple begins serving one another because it feels so good. That's what the chemical high does for them. Doing stuff for each other becomes a way of life.

- **It brings happiness into the new home.** This is like a two-year party. There's romance, lots of sex, lots of sharing, and lots of dreaming. They are living in a fairy-tale dream.
- **It brings security into the marriage.** Every time something special happens, the couple gains more confidence that this marriage is great, fantastic, and is going to last a lifetime.
- **It begins the one-ness process.** For every day that passes, for every act of service that is performed, and for every moment of celebration the couple gets closer and closer. This is intimacy building in a strong, healthy way. So, what do you think happens when a couple keeps on getting closer? Eventually they disappear into one another and become one. This is the ultimate goal. Couples in stage two have a giant head start in this process.

There are some couples that experience problems in the first two years of marriage. If you are one of those couples, don't worry. Problems came sooner to you than most couples. It's not hopeless. But just know that most couples just have a great time during those first two years of marriage. You know, before it all comes crashing …

Stage Three—The Power Struggle! This stage covers the third and fourth year of marriage. Here are some alarming statistics about the third year:

- Of the young marriages that will end, many end in the third or fourth year.
- The chemical high that is produced when a person "falls in love" lasts anywhere from 18 months to three years.
- Of those couples that live together before they marry, most will marry in the third or fourth year after moving in together, and will have a greater than 50 percent chance of divorce than couples who did not live together before marriage.
- The third year of marriage is usually the worst for many couples.

Terrified? Well, you don't have to be. Most couples who see their marriages suffer and fail during that third or fourth year of marriage don't understand what's going on. And, they don't know what to do about what they don't understand. Consequently, many opt for divorce, assuming that they just stopped loving each other, or that "it was just not meant to be," whatever that means.

Because you are reading this book, you already have an advantage over those couples whose marriages fail in this stage because you are going to learn the secrets of what's going on here. And, it's not rocket science. If I can figure it out, so can you.

The big culprits in this stage are those brain chemicals. The falling in love caused the natural secretion of those things that produced a "high in love" feeling. They made you want to DO stuff for each other, which in turn provided satisfaction of experiencing the true love. With the fading of those chemicals after about two to three years, the "wanting" or "desiring" to do stuff for each other is no longer there. It's just not as fun.

Dr. Bob Truism #6:

The marriage relationship is always FLUID. You either grow closer together or you grow further apart. Marriage is never stagnant.

The husband wakes up one morning and notices that something has changed. "I'm giving a whole lot more to this marriage than I'm getting." So, he backs away from the stuff he was doing for his wife. The wife wakes up one morning and notices the same thing. "I'm giving a whole lot more than I am getting." She also backs away from the stuff she was doing for her husband. Already, the couple has a gap in their marriage. And everyday that passes with the husband and wife doing less for each other, the gap widens. Eventually they get to the point where they don't know each other any more. They are strangers in their own home. They wonder what went wrong with their partner.

Did they stop loving each other? Yes! Remember, love is not the feeling, it is the doing. And they stopped the doing.

Now, they intentionally withdraw from each other, and all kinds of bad things fly around in their minds. They create:

- **Silent boundaries.** It's almost as if they say, "Well, if he's not going to do this, I'm not going to do this." They draw a line in the sand and dare each other to cross it. But since they are not communicating, neither knows what the other wants.

- **Verbal attacks.** "You don't love me anymore." "What was I thinking marrying you?" "You're killing our marriage." The severity of the words used suggest the severity of the feelings. By the time they get here, they are very wounded.

- **Imaginary scenarios.** The couple looks back for evidence that they missed. "I should have known she would treat me like dirt because of what happened that day on the beach." "He hates me. He's probably looking for someone else right now." Once the mind starts wandering in imaginary land the couple's problems continue to increase.

- **Impossible standards.** Both will imagine a standard the other must reach before they can feel confident to love again. The standards are set high.

"Whenever she decides to do _____
then I'll do_____ ." But, again,
since neither is talking to the other, neither knows
about the standards and both will continue to fail.

By the way, if all this trouble is caused by couples
who stop serving one another, what is the solution to the
problem? Start serving each other again! Half of your
problems will simply go away. We can help you work on
the other issues.

Here's another thing that goes wrong during this time,
and it has to do with those "high in love" chemicals. When
a person falls in love, they don't become blind as in "love is
blind." What happens is that each CHOOSES to ignore the
faults and irritating habits of the other. They feel too good
to bother with such triviality. But when the high wears
off, they CHOOSE not to ignore those faults any longer. If
this is true, what's the solution to this problem? CHOOSE
again to overlook each other's faults. Those irritating
habits are only irritating when you keep dwelling on them
with negativity. Stop it!

The problems that arise during this stage are easily
understood. The solution to the problems is easily seen.
The hardest part is getting the couple to do what they are
supposed to do. The chemical high is no longer there.
Something else must motivate the couple to serve each
other. Marital commitment must be that motivation. If

the couple will choose to serve one another again, good feelings that come because of service will return. If a couple can do these things, and make it through the third and fourth year of marriage, they have a great chance of making it "… 'til death do us part."

Stage Four—The Daily Grind! This stage generally covers the fourth through the tenth years of marriage. Couples in this stage realize that making a marriage work requires constant attention and lots of hard work. They no longer try to change the other person, or worry so much about why the other person isn't changing, they just start working hard for each other. This is the stage in which children start showing up. Mom and dad need to get along so the kids can have a happy home in which to grow up. The healthy couple sees the importance of serving each other and starts putting more energy into it.

And speaking of energy, here's a strange fact. Did you know that it takes less energy to serve someone than it does to be served? In other words, you actually expend more energy sitting around waiting to be served than if you got up and did some act of service. Why? Because, when you choose to be a servant (not a slave) you get to choose what you do, when to do it, how often, and the duration of the act of service. You are in control. There is no stress. But when you wait to be served, you will

NEVER be satisfied. The one serving you will either not do it exactly as you desire, not do it often enough, or not do everything you wish. Lots of stress enters your mind and heart. Misery follows. Maybe that's why many kings in history went crazy towards the end of their lives. They were miserable sitting around waiting to be served. When you concentrate all of your energy on yourself, you will always be miserable.

Consider the story of John D. Rockefeller, Sr. I heard this on one of Paul Harvey's "The rest of the story." It seems that as chairman of the great Standard Oil Trust in the 1800s he was one of the wealthiest men in the world as well as a much-hated man. He was known to have pressured other oil companies into selling to him or face being forced into bankruptcy. The oil workers in the field would burn effigies of Rockefeller to show their hatred of him. Wealth and power came to this man, but not peace of mind. It seems that when Rockefeller was 53 years old he was close to death. He was able only to eat crackers with water. On the night he thought he was to die, he had a brilliant thought. He realized that he could not take any of his wealth with him. So that night he determined that, if he would live another day, he would begin to give his great wealth away. He survived that night and did as promised. The University of Chicago was founded. Millions went into medical research. The money Rockefeller donated to medical science is credited with the eradication of hookworm and yellow fever in America. The Rockefeller Foundation today is still one of the greatest charities in the world. Because he started giving away his fortune, John D. Rockefeller, Sr. survived his 53rd year, and the 54th and 55th year of life. He finally did die ... one month shy of his 98th birthday.

Selfishness destroys. Selflessness makes you strong and healthy.

Stage Five—Shaping Up. This stage covers the tenth through the twenty-fifth year of marriage. It is at this time that the couple begins to realize that each has unique gifts that they bring to the marriage and the family. The couple rallies together to present a united front against the issues that arise during this stage. The kids are getting older and require more attention. Careers take more time. Bills are greater. Retirement is not too far away. If the couple does not become stronger during this time, they will be torn apart.

The biggest issue here is definitely the kids. Children are born into this world selfish. They demand comfort whenever they are uncomfortable. They cry when they want food, clean diapers, and sleep. And as they grow, they attempt to remain selfish and resist the demands of the parents to "Just grow up!" They continue to practice what they learned in the infant and toddler stages—how to play mommy against daddy to get their way. Then come the teenage years. Hormones are rampant. Each teen believes he/she has arrived at the level of maturity that should allow them to be on their own, with you providing for all the expenses, of course. Teenagers, a lot of the time, are grumpy, miserable, and horrible to the parents. They truly believe that you are the stupidest people who ever walked the face of the earth.

So we fight back with the parental speeches. "Don't you talk to your father that way! Treat him with respect!" "Do you think that if all your friends jumped off the edge of a cliff that you would too?" or "When you have kids of your own I hope they are JUST LIKE YOU!" All we seem to do with teenagers is make them mad. And all they seem to do is make us mad. If the married couple does not band together, they will be torn apart.

Try this the next time your teen smarts off to you. Give them some empathy, then some consequences. They won't know what hit them. Let's say your teen says this: "I don't know why I can't go out tonight. You're so stupid!" Instead of getting mad, say this in an empathetic voice: "Oooooo, that's soooooo sad. You must be feeling awful to talk that way to me. Oooooo, that's sooooo sad. And that was sure a bad decision you made to call me stupid. Ooooooooooooo. Well, that took away all of my energy. So

I guess you'll have to do these chores for me." Then present the teen with a list of three to ten chores. The empathy disarmed the situation. You did not get mad so the teen did not win. Plus you gave him/her consequences for their disrespectful behavior. (For more on this way of handling kids of all ages, find a Parenting with Love and Logic® workshop in your area.)

Couples who do band together during this stage of marriage realize that marriage doesn't have to be so hard. It can be a lot of fun. The kids will soon be gone and they can look forward to another honeymoon stage.

My wife and I, as I write this book, have one child left at home. Though we are in the sixth stage of marriage, we are still working hard at presenting a united front against the teenage persona living in our home. He will be off to college in just a few months. We are looking forward to it. In fact, we're going to have a party.

Marriage can be a lot of fun. It gets even better when your kids have kids. There are two main reasons grandkids are so much fun. First, you get to play with them and spoil them and give them back. And, they DO turn out JUST LIKE THEM.

Stage Six—Two Become One. This stage covers the 25th year of marriage and beyond. When a couple keeps getting closer and closer each year that passes, the natural result is that someday they will disappear into one another. They become one. This doesn't mean that they are no longer individuals with rights of their own. But what it does mean is that they know that serving another brings the greatest rewards in life. The couple's attitude gets more and more tuned in to the other's needs and wants. It's a great time of life.

Stage Six is the best and most satisfying time of life. There are too many things to enjoy, so why waste time worrying about the small things that younger couples worry about? There are grandkids to play with. There are adventures to experience. Older couples enjoy a great sense of humor. They have the greatest stories just to laugh about or to use to help younger people understand life.

Couples in this stage of life become experts in pure love. Remember the definition? It is "doing stuff for each other." Older married folks love to give and serve. They are experts!

I remember a few years ago that my daughter called me up, crying about a bill that she received. She was a grown up, young adult, already out of college, working at her first job. She was still my daughter so her crying broke my heart. It seems that during the Christmas season she worked part-time for a store just to make some extra money. She didn't make enough money for the company to take out income taxes. In April she learned she owed the IRS $600. Thus the phone call and the crying.

I remember at the time of that call I was unemployed. My unemployment came as a surprise to me so I wasn't prepared. But I did have $600 in my savings account. After talking with her for a while I told her that I would loan her the money. I impressed upon her that I was not employed and that I needed the money back as soon as possible.

Question: Do you believe that I will ever see that money ever again? No. Do you think I will ever remind my daughter of this loan? No. Why? Because I'm an expert at pure love. I knew when I loaned her the money that it was really a gift. And I gave it without expecting anything in return. (Krista, if you are reading this book, don't feel one bit guilty and do not try to pay me back. We're doing okay. Remember, I'm an expert at this. Love you!)

My older son is a member of the Oregon Air National Guard. As a Tech Sergeant, he deals with the avionics on the F-15 fighter jets that roar in and out of the Portland OR air base. He makes a good living, in fact he makes more right now than I do. But on Sundays, when we go out to eat after church, who pays for dinner? I do. I'm the expert. Every once in a while my son tries to wrestle the check out of my hand. And, every once in a while I let him win. But I tell him, "I like to pay for dinner. Let me pay."

Here's the best part of Stage Six. Since a healthy marriage makes you happy and healthy, marriage is actually a gift. In fact, the greatest gift you could ever give to your spouse is to have a happy marriage. Look forward to a long lasting marriage. Put some effort into in and you will find that it gets better and better each year.

Stage Seven—Precious Memories. This is the stage of marriage that we don't want to think about. This is the time of life when one of the marriage partners dies. We still call this a stage of marriage because married love does not stop here. Love does not die. It keeps going. It becomes stronger and elevates the love and the lover to the level of a champion. It changes, and takes on a whole new dynamic.

When a husband or wife dies, the survivor is forced to change the way he/she loves. Love is no longer face-to-face. Love is now in memories. So the stories are told. Friends, family, children and grandchildren are told of the amazing love that one man had for one woman. The stories bring hope and guidance to future generations. In this way, married love continues.

Death has an amazing way of filtering love, too. We usually remember only the good things. We usually share only those stories that will lift and encourage someone. Love, in memories, can be stronger than it was in life. And it keeps going.

There is this couple I know, Heston and Ruth Havens, that keep falling deeper in love every year that they are married. On June 2, 2008 they celebrated their 70th wedding anniversary. To me they represent the epitome of love. If ever a couple illustrated the beauty of the one-ness process, it would be them. I could have used this story in the last section, in Stage Six, where two become one. But there is a beautiful reason I have included this story here. You'll cry. I warn you.

When I was a minister in Portland, we would have a yearly family retreat. During that retreat, we would have a talent show. And, every year, Heston and Ruth would get up and recite a poem to each other. It was so beautiful. It was so sweet.

Heston told me that they started reciting this poem to each other, in public, over 50 years ago. The poem was entitled "Should You Go First." It was written by a master orator named A.K. Rowswell, the "Voice of the Pittsburg Pirates." Rowswell, who died in 1955, published two books of poetry. This poem was his most famous.

You will be impressed by this poem. It speaks of a couple in which one or both are nearing death. They are preparing to continue loving one another after death.

I took my camera to Heston and Ruth's home. I asked if they could recite the poem for me so I could share it in our workshops.

I hadn't seen them in a couple of years. Ruth had taken a fall that affected her memory. Neither could recite the poem by memory any longer. With copies of the poem in their hands, they gave it their all.

I turned on the camera and asked them what their secret was to a long and happy marriage. Heston said, "... self-less-ness is the key." He also said, "50/50 doesn't work, at least not right. It takes a 100 percent effort from both to have a good marriage ... and that we've enjoyed."

Then, with a little prompting, Ruth began. Her voice was steady and sure. She read the first four lines of the poem. Heston would follow with another four lines. How did they finish the poem? With a kiss, of course. The video of this wonderful couple is a permanent part of our marriage workshops. I wish every couple could have the love they have!

Heston and Ruth are still living and enjoying life. But one day one will die before the other. But they have already decided what they will do. They will keep their love alive through memories and through sharing stories of married love. What a wonderful way to complete life.

What Does a 'Problem' Really Look Like?

KNOWLEDGE IS THE KEY! To be able to resolve a problem we must know what a problem looks like. If we don't have this knowledge, we may spend lots of our time and energy doing the wrong things to try to fix problems and getting undesired results. In this chapter we are going to dissect a problem. Once we cut it open we will see how it started, how it advanced, how it got way out of hand, and how it got worse by improper handling.

So I'm in my bedroom after mowing the lawn. I am shedding clothing in preparation for a shower. I throw my two socks at the clothes hamper. One of them goes in, one of them hits the floor. I walk away not thinking too much about it. My wife sees this event and says, "Hey, pick up your sock." I sense a little parental-overbearing-ness in her voice. So I react and say, "You pick it up." Well, she doesn't like what she hears and she says in a bit louder voice, "It's your sock. Pick it up!" To which I reply, "You're closer. You pick it up!" For the next few minutes we both are cleverly crafting zinger statements designed to get the other to bow in submission and do the deed that isn't being done. After a while I say something incredibly stupid like, "You pick it up, it's woman's work anyway." She has no reply. But she stomps out of the room and slams the door. I go off to the bathroom and slam my door. Then we don't speak to one another for about three days. Neither of us wants to break the silence and thus lose this earthshaking argument. We do speak again only when another sock-on-the-floor-like incident occurs. And then it's just another world war in our home.

So here we are, a good, loving married couple, at the brink of divorce over what—a sock on the floor? Now, I'm a level-headed man. I figure the problem can be resolved very easily. I'll go pick up the sock, which is still in place, on the floor outside the hamper in the bedroom. Fine! End of story! But that just doesn't work. My wife sees all kinds of other issues that also must be talked about.

To get this problem resolved we must see all the different aspects of the problem and resolve every one of them. If we try to correct the smaller actions, like tossing a sock on the floor or slamming a door, but don't resolve the three days of silence, the problem will never be resolved. And, if we try to come up with a compromise without discussing the heated words that were exchanged, the problem cannot be resolved. You can see already that the problem has almost outgrown the couple. So let's open it up and see what's inside. Understanding the problem is half the battle. The other half of the problem can be resolved with healthy communication.

First—Every Problem Begins with Selfishness. Selfishness is when one thinks only of himself. It also causes him to look down with spite on the thoughts and feelings of another.

Back to the incident with the sock on the floor. How did it start? I say it was innocent. It was an accident. My aim wasn't as good as it should have been. Accidents happen. But the real problem began when I walked away from the sock, not caring about what was right or decent. I was in my own la-la-land. Selfishness, because I only thought about myself, started the problem.

But selfishness also adds to the problem and distorts it. My wife joined in and helped the matter grow out of proportion. She also began innocently. She saw an injustice and offered words that would correct the situation, "Hey, pick up your sock." Now, I've already admitted to being selfish at the beginning of the problem. But I made it worse by reacting to my wife's words because they offended me. Selfishness made me snap back at her.

My wife also entered the arena of selfishness by snapping back at me.

Let's stop here for a moment. What could I have done to keep this problem from getting out of hand? I could have just picked up the sock. This would have truly been the end of the story. And, what could my wife have done, if she wanted, to keep this problem from getting out of hand? She could have picked up the sock for me. This would have truly been the end of the story. If this is so easy, why did neither of us choose the high road? Selfishness!

What did selfishness make us do? We snapped at each other. We put each other down. We looked at each other with contempt. We even used bad language and filthy names. Why? Selfishness, selfishness, selfishness, and selfishness.

But it didn't stop there. We continued our selfish tirades by stomping out and slamming doors. And, yes, selfishness was the attitude that caused the three days of silence between us. We both are guilty. I started the problem, but we both added to it.

Most couples become experts on making problems bigger than they should. Here are some of the "expert" behaviors that accompany most marital arguments:

- **Unkind words**— This includes but is not limited to cursing and swearing, comparing one's spouse to an animal or at least the rear end of certain barnyard equines, and demeaning each other's state of mind.

- **Raising the voice**— Surely if your spouse didn't listen to your criticism when you first used your soft indoor voice, he/she will listen if you raise the volume a few decibels. Right? Not! If I don't speak Spanish, you can yell at me all you want in Spanish and I still won't understand.

- **Name calling**— This is a third-grade defense mechanism. You remember third grade? A kid cannot match wits with another. So he comes out with some insult that will surely end the argument. Here's how it usually goes: "Bobby got in trouble. Bobby got in trouble." To which Bobby would reply, "Oh yeah? Well, you're stupid!" Once you get to the name calling stage, you are no longer smarter than a third grader.

- **Facial expressions**— Couples can get very creative here. There's the ever popular eye-rolling, the pursed lips, the "look", or the stoic martyrs look, you know the Joan of Arc solemn stare as she faces her fate of being burned at the stake even though she knows she's totally innocent. Some couples should get awards for their attempts to silently slaughter their opponents with facial contortions.

Second—Every problem usually ends up bigger than it should. We've already seen this happen with the sock incident. But let's put labels on what happened. Think of the problem as an iceberg. They say that only about 12% of an iceberg is in plain view above the water. That means there is seven times as much ice floating below the surface of the water. That hidden ice is what is so dangerous to the ocean liners. In our illustration of a problem, the tip of the problem is what we call the action. This is what really happened. It is the true problem that began as a small conflict. This is the tip of the iceberg.

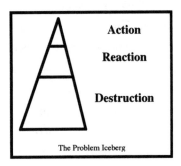

The Problem Iceberg

We make the problem even bigger by what we add to it. This is the reaction. There are all kinds of things we use to blow a conflict way out of proportion.

- **Hateful words**— "Well, that was brilliant!" "Have you lost your mind?" "Are you blind?" "No matter what I do you always get mad at me." "Nag, nag, nag." (Put your own phrase here: "_____
_____ .")

- **Voice volume**— Gets louder and louder as the argument progresses.

- **Name calling**— Can't put here what couples really call each other. Otherwise we'd have to put an 'R' rating on this book.
- **Facial expressions**— Rolling the eyes, blank stare, "The Look!"
- **Prehistoric grunts**— Sighs, growls, "tsk, tsk, tsk"
- **Mumbling under your breath**— Loud enough for the other to hear that you are muttering about something but soft enough so they don't hear what you are really saying.

All these additions to the original problem are categorized as the "reaction" to the problem. Already it seems as if the problem has gotten out of hand.

Then there's the "destruction" of the problem. It's like the silence after a bomb goes off. The couple is dazed and confused. They spend time apart not talking to each other. In our example the couple does not talk for three days. This is not a cooling-off period as some want to suggest. This is a continuation of the problem. The couple doesn't really cool down, they continue to fester, in their own corners, about the hurt and the hate that the other displayed during the action and reaction stage of the problem. So the problem just keeps on growing. If a couple ever has a chance to resolve conflicts in marriage, they need to recognize the total aspect of the problem and address all levels.

Third—unresolved past problems make all new problems difficult to resolve. Did you know that every conflict that you have ever had in your marriage that has not been successfully resolved is still with you? It just floats above your heads in a cloud. Over time the cloud can become very thick and dark. All those past unresolved problems are just right there to use against each other. This is a big problem because it happens all the time.

Let's go back to our illustration. I threw a sock on the floor and failed to pick it up. Now, my wife and I are trying to come up with sharp statements designed to make the other give in. "You pick it up, it's your sock!" "You pick it up, you're closer." But if none of these masterpieces of rhetoric works, couples may dig into the cloud and pull out a past indiscretion. "Well, I guess I can't expect you to pick up your socks. You never seem to be able to pick up the newspaper after you read it." "Oh yeah, we'll you're not so perfect. I don't know when the last time the kitchen was clean!" What happened here? Is this right? Does this help? The answers are "no" and "never". Why do couples resort to bringing up the past in conflicts?

- Because every new problem stirs up the ill feelings of all past unresolved problems. Those past issues have created "concepts" in marriage. Distrust, disappointment, and discouragement are just a few. So, when a new problem arises in marriage, a couple may look at it through these filters. There may be an automatic distrust that my partner will not handle the new issue correctly, so I will look at the issue as hopeless, no matter how small it may be. This is not fair to your partner. This is also called "prejudice" because you have prejudged one another. This just messes everything up.

- Because couples tend to use past unresolved problems as weapons to keep from getting hurt. If the sock-thrower feels like he is being backed into a corner, he may lash out at his wife with other past events to keep from feeling the guilt of his error and to keep from feeling the wrath of his wife. This doesn't work. He's still in a corner, his wife is still angry, and he feels awful.

- Because couples cannot or refuse to center their discussion on one single issue, thus making all problems impossible to resolve. Problems or conflicts enter marriage one at a time. Then we muddy the waters by bringing up other conflicts. Now we have this big wad of intertwined problems that cannot possibly be resolved. Eventually, the couple may forget what the real issue was. It was a "sock on the floor." And, the couple may actually not care anymore about the real issue since they are now stewing over all the garbage that has been brought up. How can this ever be resolved?

- Because unresolved problems have already caused both partners to devalue the other. In a healthy marriage, partners should have this attitude: "My husband/wife is so valuable to me that I will do anything to make him/her happy." But because of the couple's inability to resolve any problem, both have devalued the other. And, what's the opposite of "value?" Worthless!

Are you beginning to get the picture that unresolved problems multiply the hurt of all marital problems? Do you think it might be important to resolve all problems as they come up? "But what if I've been married for 30 years? What if I have hundreds of unresolved problems in my marriage?" Keep reading. We'll show you how.

Fourth—the language barrier between the sexes makes problem resolution difficult. Men, for the most part, are cognitive in their outlook on life. They speak the cognitive language. Women, for the most part, are affective in their outlook on life. They speak the affective language. One writer said that men are from Mars and women are from Venus. That's corny. Aren't Mars and Venus a million miles away from each other? Sometimes when couples try to talk about problems it's as if they are a million miles away from each other. If we don't talk the same language, we can never resolve a problem.

Let me use a non-marital example to illustrate this concept. Let's say I was in my office with my a man who speaks only Spanish. I speak only English. I notice that his car is on fire in the parking lot. So I say, in English, "Your car is on fire in the parking lot. Go get the fire extinguisher and put it out." He also notices that his car is on fire and says to me, in Spanish, "¡Bob, mi carro! Necesito a extinguir el fuego! ¿Tienes un extintor?" I just sit there, staring at him, not knowing what in the world he said. I figure he wasn't listening. So I speak louder, and slower, in English, hoping that my loud English will get through to his Spanish ears. So I say, "YOUR CAR IS ON FIRE IN THE PARKING LOT! GO GET THE FIRE EXTINGUISHER AND PUT IT OUT!" My loud, slow English comes across as demeaning to him, and that's probably how I intended it. He just looks at me, staring at me, not knowing what in the world I was saying to him. He just knows I'm not being very nice to him. He returns the favor by repeating what he said, a little slower, and a lot louder. "¡BOB, MI CARRO! NECESITO A EXTINGUIR EL FUEGO! ¿TIENES UN EXTINTOR?" Now I'm ticked off. We are about ready to slug each other.

Think about this: We are saying the same thing! We believe the same way about the same thing. But because we are speaking in a language the other does not understand, we are getting ready to kill each other. This is exactly what happens in marriage. We don't speak the same language. And instead of learning the other's language, we just look down on our mates and ridicule them for not being like us. The language barrier makes conflict resolution almost impossible.

The Bible story of the Tower of Babel is the perfect study in communication. After the Great Flood, mankind was supposed to spread out over all the earth to repopulate what the flood destroyed. The people, rather than obey the command of God, settled in a nice valley and built a city. In their eagerness to create a long-lasting society in that area they also built a tower that would reach into the heavens. God did not like what He saw. He spoke to Christ and the Holy Spirit about it one day. "Behold, they are one people, and they all have the same language. And this is what they began to do, and now nothing which they purpose to do will be impossible for them" *(Genesis 11:6)*. God said that when men speak the same language, they can do anything they set their mind to. But He didn't want the people to settle in that area. He needed to scatter the people throughout the earth. How could God possibly accomplish that? He could have raised up an enemy army to march against God's people and chase them to the four corners of the earth. Or He could have sent locust to do the same. But instead, God confused their language. "Come, let *Us* go down and confuse their language that they may not understand one another's speech" *(Genesis 11:7)*. This is how God scattered the people. If you speak the same language, you can do anything. But if you don't speak the same language, you can do nothing.

Whoa! That's a lot to drink in. Problems get bigger than they should and get even worse because of communication breakdowns. Since men and women speak different languages, what are we supposed to do? How can we ever get our problems resolved?

Give yourself a pat on the back for defogging your marriage a little bit more. Understanding the problem is half the battle. In a couple of chapters you will learn an effective conflict resolution tool. And this tool will help resolve the problem, the whole problem, and nothing but the problem. Here's what will happen:

1. Problem resolution will have a service component. If every problem begins with selfishness, then problem resolution begins with service. "What can I DO for my spouse that will help this problem get resolved?"

2. Both parties will have a spirit of humility. You've tried it in the past; it won't work, you know, when you tried to make the other person understand what they've done wrong. The right way is to come with a humble spirit, believing that both of you have participated in this problem. With the right attitude, anything can be accomplished.

3. You will address problems one at a time. They entered your marriage one at a time and will have to leave one at a time. But don't worry, they will all disappear quickly.

4. You will address problems in a controlled atmosphere. Free-for-alls don't work. You will center in on one problem, get it resolved, and throw it out of your marriage.

5. You will address all three stages of the problem: the action, the reaction, and the destruction. Again, don't worry, it'll be easy once you understand, once the fog lifts.

6. You will develop a basic understanding of your mate's language. This can be fun. The cognitive partner will learn the affective language and the affective partner will learn the cognitive language.

7. You will fix the problem! Men, for the most part, need this.

8. You will address the emotions surrounding the problem. Women, for the most part, need this.

9. You will communicate as equals. If you have ever tried to resolve a problem when the other is feeling superior to you, it doesn't go well. You are husband and wife. You are not father and daughter, or mother and son. You are equal partners in the wonderful life called marriage.

Understanding Your Temperament Differences

KNOWLEDGE IS THE KEY. There is something created inside all of us that may be different than what is inside my mate. Temperament. If I can understand my mate's temperament, then I can have more patience and better communicate. If I don't understand temperament differences, I may begin to assume that he/she is just being difficult.

I never could understand my wife. We would go to the mall and she would want to spend hours going from store to store, just looking, and eventually buying the thing she wanted. Why couldn't she just go straight to the store, buy the thing, and get out? That's what I would do. What's wrong with her?

What's wrong with him? We make a special trip to go to the mall and he just wants to run in and run out. Why can't he enjoy the atmosphere, enjoy ME walking hand in hand with him? He lets me know how much he hates the mall. Finally I give up and get out of there.

Has this ever happened to you? Have you ever felt there was something seriously wrong with your mate because he/she would not enjoy what you enjoy? Because of this, have you assigned a not-so-kind name for your mate like butthead, killjoy, or some other name not appropriate for this book? It might be that these are temperament differences. Here are some more:

- You like making new friends but your mate is antisocial.
- You need to talk about problems, right away, with energy, but your mate just shuts down.
- You want to talk but you have to drag information out of your spouse.
- Your mate always seems to be right and makes you believe that you are garbage.
- Your mate wants to go, go, go all the time, but he/she won't slow down long enough to have a good conversation with you.
- Your mate wants to argue with everyone but you just want peace.
- Your mate never wants to make a decision.
- Your mate wants to make all the decisions.

- Your mate can get real angry real quick about a matter, and then forgets about it just as quickly. But you can't get over it.
- Your mate never wants to initiate lovemaking. What's wrong with him/her?

These statements could just be male/female differences, or they may indicate normal temperament differences between the husband and wife. Your mate is not necessarily being difficult; he/she may just be living their temperament.

Temperament has nothing to do with anger. It is a description of your attitude or outlook on life and relationships. You were born with it. It's why you do what you do. It's why you react in certain ways to conflict and pain. If you can understand temperament, you can better talk to your mate and better resolve conflicts.

The science of temperament has been around for centuries. And, it hasn't changed much over time. In fact, some of the same words used two or three thousand years ago are still used today: melancholy, choleric, and sanguine. So it's a pretty exact science, and it is used widely by mental health professionals and employers. Some of the more widely used temperament tests are:

- **MMPI**— Minnesota Multiphasic Personality Inventory
- **MBTI**— Myers-Briggs Type Indicator

- **APS or TAPs**— Arno Profile System or Temperament Analysis Profile

Some writers use nontechnical terms to educate their readers about the four major temperament types. They may use:
- **Colors**— Gold, Blue, Orange, Green
- **Animals**— Golden retriever, Otter, Lion, Beaver
- **Descriptive words**— Peacemaker, Partier, Pusher, Protector

In this chapter we will use the descriptive words. They are my creation. I don't want to infringe on anyone's copyrights.

Here's what you need to do. Read all the temperament descriptions below. Decide which one of them best describes you. Then, decide which one of them, at least in your opinion, best describes your mate. After this, read the section on the unique needs of each temperament. Focus more on your mate's needs—what you can do for him/her.

The Temperaments

The Protector!

We call them protectors because of their enormous desire to protect what is right. These people are enforcers of rules. They are usually on-time to everything and become stressed when they are late. They are protectors of their emotions, rarely sharing them with others. Protectors don't have many close friends. When conflict arises, they will protect their feelings by shutting down. They keep their feeling to themselves until such a time when they feel the need to explode. Protectors don't have much of a mood swing. They are fairly reserved most of the time. They usually look at the negative side of everything, and can usually figure out what can possibly go wrong.

Protectors are deep thinkers. They are brilliant. They know what you need to do with your life and will tell you IF you come and ask them for advice. They must process information before acting upon it. If allowed to think about a certain matter, they can do it well. If forced into making a quick decision about something they haven't thought about, they will rebel and shut down.

Protectors are defenders of deep relationships. They will, if needed, give the ultimate sacrifice, their own life, for another.

The Peacemaker!

Peacemakers are gentle and sweet. They are humble and loving. They enjoy watching others take the spotlight. But they have a hard time making decisions because of how it might affect others. They would rather that someone else decide for them, even if the decision affects them personally. While protectors will rebel and shut down to avoid conflict, peacemakers will do anything to make peace, even give up their rights for others. This is noble. But if peacemakers are not careful they can become doormats for others to walk on. Peacemakers defer to others so often they have difficulty saying what's on their hearts. Because of this, peacemakers expect others to read their minds. But since no one can do this, many of their needs go unmet.

Peacemakers have an enormous desire for social interaction, but need to be invited so they know the friendship is true and genuine. They may use a lot of indirect behavior. They try to hint to others what is going on inside them, in hopes that others will come and ask, "What's wrong?" or "Do you want to come with us?"

Peacemakers are very humble and have a hard time accepting compliments. They often feel worthless and unworthy of any recognition. But they secretly enjoy the attention.

The Pusher!

If we didn't have pushers in the world, nothing would get done. Pushers and Protectors have the same ability to see the big picture, to know what others need to do. Yes, Pushers are brilliant, too. While Protectors are more than willing to give advice if someone comes to them and asks, Pushers not only know what you should do with your life, they have an overwhelming need to push you to do what you need to do.

Pushers are good leaders and are good at delegating responsibilities, empowering others to perform good tasks. They can be personable and persuasive. However, if they are not successful in pushing others using enlightenment and persuasion, they may use not-so-good behaviors to accomplish what they want—anger, manipulation, or coercion. Pushers have a hard time sharing feelings. They will not allow others to help them make decisions.

They like social situations. But they often will use socialization as a way to get ahead or to make another sale—networking.

The Partier!

These are the people who love life. They want to be involved in everything that is good, and fun. They love using all five senses all the time. They love the aesthetic beauty in all things. They love to shop and spend money. They like to buy decorative things, knickknacks, jars and vases.

Partiers enjoy life. They are usually in charge of the conversation and usually the loudest in the room. If they find themselves getting bored, they may move on to someone or something else. They may leave in the middle of a conversation just to find someone or something else more entertaining. They love music and conversation. Sometimes they have the radio and TV going while talking on the telephone. Partiers have extreme mood swings. But they are either way up or way down, almost never in the middle. When they notice they are coming down from the emotional high because of conflict, they may take on bad behaviors to keep themselves on the emotional high.

Partiers have many friends and a good number of close friends. It's because they enjoy people. They are like sunshine on a cloudy day.

Temperament—
What does your Partner need?

If you are married to a Protector ...

Your Protector spouse will shut down at the first sign of conflict. Your approach should be wrapped with a lot of gentleness. If you ask, "What's wrong?" and he/she says, "Nothing!" then leave him/her alone until enough time passes for them to process the situation. It would be good to set an appointment. "Honey, do you think we could talk about this at 5:00 tonight?" Protectors understand appointments and rules.

Your Protector does not enjoy social situations as other temperaments do. They are mostly uncomfortable and prefer being in small groups IF they know and are comfortable with them. Any pressure towards socializing will produce stress. Even if your protector eventually gives in and agrees to go, he/she will carry a lot of stress to the social engagement.

They don't like to be surprised. It would be better for you to make an appointment to talk about serious matters ("Do you think maybe we can talk at 5:00 tonight?") rather than forcing the issue immediately ("We've got to talk about this now!"). Protectors must have time to process information.

Your Protector values schedules and time frames. If he/she knows the starting and stopping point of any event, they are more comfortable participating. For example, don't ask, "Honey, do you want to go to the mall?" Your Protector will freeze and panic because there is not enough information to make a decision. Instead ask, "Honey, do you want to go to the mall for an hour?" Instead of, "Do you want to go for a walk?" say, "Do you want to walk to the store and back?"

Your Protector can be a fantastic lover. He/she has deep emotions and wants to share them. But they also have a great fear of rejection. For this reason they may appear uninterested in love and intimacy. In reality, they are waiting, observing, and responding to you as you initiate the romantic encounter. So, welcome his/her romantic interests and advances. If you must decline, do it in a gentle way. "Honey, I would love to, but I just can't tonight. Do you think we can do it tomorrow night?"

The appearance of competency is very important to your Protector. Be sure to allow him/her to be in a favorable light in front of others.

One of the greatest needs of your Protector is encouragement. Tell him/her often that you are proud of them. Thank them for their efforts. Congratulate their successes. A happy Protector is a fantastic mate.

If you are married to a Peacemaker ...

Your Peacemaker spouse will also shut down at the first sign of conflict. Their "shut down" is because they don't know how to share their feelings effectively. But they want so badly to share with you. They secretly need you to draw their feelings out of them. If you ask, "Honey, what's wrong?" and he/she says "Nothing?" what they are really saying is "Please keep asking me." Peacemakers want you to read their mind. But since you can't, just remember to keep asking and they will eventually tell you what's going on, how they're feeling. Set aside quality time for them to open up and share their feelings.

Your peacemaker will often display indirect behavior. If you don't read minds, your peacemaker will throw out hints to get you to draw them out. These hints can look like facial expressions, sighs and other nonverbal grunts, as not-so-well-crafted statements and questions. "Must be nice to go to Macy's." You need to reassure them they are valuable and loved.

Peacemakers enjoy social events. They need personal invitations so they know that they are needed or wanted at the event. But even in social situations, your Peacemaker will be more of an observer than a participant. So be sure to stay with them and include them in your conversations.

Your Peacemaker is a deep lover. Their nature suggests that they want only the best for others. But they are more responders than initiators. So take the time to initiate intimacy with your Peacemaker mate. If done gently, they will open up and share fantastic love with you.

One of the greatest needs of your Peacemaker is attention. Pay lots of attention. Ask lots of questions. Though they don't want to make decisions, include your mate in any decision making process. They want to touch and be touched (nonsexual, like hugs, pat on the back, stroking the arm, etc.) So, touch them!

If you are married to a Pusher...

Your Pusher is a very brilliant person. He/she can see the big picture and what needs to be done. Conflict is not distasteful for them. But they will use it to get others to do what they are supposed to do. If they can't, they may display anger in an attempt to motivate or move others. They are right much of the time, but they are pushy. So, if you feel overwhelmed by your Pusher, tell him/her, "Honey, I know you're probably right, but I'm feeling overwhelmed. Can you give me some space or some time?"

Even when gentle, it is important to stand up to the Pusher. If not, they tend to overwhelm people then lose respect for them. So, for their sake, stand up to them in conflict and resolve all issues in healthy ways.

Your Pusher enjoys social situations. He/she looks at them as opportunities for advancement. Appearance is important to them. Be gracious and attentive in public.

Pushers hate to be vulnerable, but they need to open up and share feelings just like anyone else. Provide for them a place where they can feel safe.

One of the greatest needs of the Pusher is encouragement. And this is tough. Since your Pusher is often right and uses situations to advance his/her own agenda, he/she can become arrogant. But even with arrogance, they are secretly crying out for validation. Spend a lot of time saying, "Good job! Atta boy! I'm proud of you!"

If you are married to a Partier …

Your Partier has the overwhelming desire to always be up, positive, enjoying the moment or the day. Help him/

her enjoy life. Help provide opportunities for them to be social. They are not concerned with time schedules. If you need to approach a Partier to let them know it's time to go, do it gently then give them time to wind down from the social atmosphere.

Your Partier does not like conflict, but will not back down when conflict arises. He/she will be quick to vent emotions during conflict as a defense mechanism to keep them from falling into a negative mood. Don't, at first, take what they say as a personal attack on you, but do realize they need to resolve conflict quickly so they can stay up in the positive moods.

Provide safe places for them to be vulnerable. Listen intently to their stories. Don't correct their exaggerations. Remember, they are telling the more emotional side of the story rather than the factual side.

Your Partier's greatest need is beauty. They enjoy observing beautiful people and beautiful things. And, they enjoy sharing these things with their loving mate. Help them by orchestrating events, activities, and vacations that take you to beautiful places. Appreciate their spirit and energy.

Partiers are great lovers. They enjoy the romance and the build up to intimacy and sexual encounters. It's just another party, but this one's special and intimate.

Why all this discussion about temperaments?

1. **Understand your own temperament.** What you read here are general tendencies that you may have. The behaviors described here are comfortable. But it doesn't mean that they are always right and proper. In marriage you have agreed to share your life with another who speaks differently (Men are from Mars ...) and who reacts differently to life situations. Knowing your temperament will help you figure out how to go beyond your comfort zone for the sake of your mate.

2. **Understand your mate's temperament.** In many marital conflicts your mate is not just being difficult; your mate may just be behaving in a way that is comfortable, the way they were made. Be more patient with your mate, providing for them things and situations that will help them live within their temperaments and allow for less stress in their lives.

3. **Enjoy the differences!** They just make life more interesting. Allow your mate's strengths to fill in for your weaknesses and be the strength for those areas in which your mate is weak. Then, enjoy how strong your marriage will become.

PART III

Tools to Keep the Fog Out

C*E*A*S*E Fighting–
A Conflict Resolution Tool

OK, NOW IT'S TIME TO GET BUSY. It's time to get to work. You know you have a lot of past unresolved problems hanging over your marriage. The fog will lift once you start getting rid of the problems. In this chapter you will learn an effective way to resolve any problem big or small, past or present. But like any tool, you have to use it to get some good out of it.

From my email inbox ...
Hi, Bob,

My husband Terry and I were at the Shilo Inn, Seaside workshop on May 16th and had a great time. Thank you so much for all the practical stuff you gave us. We actually went to the workshop with some baggage from the weekend before and immediately after we got to our room, we sat in the comfy chairs and worked through the CEASE fighting steps. It was so amazing! Normally we have a hard time discussing conflict, but we worked it all out and were totally satisfied when we were through. Thank you so much!!! Now we are working on the homework. We have a date to meet each Monday and talk about the homework we did that week. It is great. We are about to work on our faithfulness plan. Thanks again and all the best to you. —Ariel

Before you begin resolving all of your marriage conflicts, let's put it into perspective—as perspective you can embrace. If it is true that every problem you have ever had, that has never been resolved, is still with you, you may have a very thick cloud hanging over your marriage. But don't be alarmed. Don't be overwhelmed. Think Mine Sweeper.

Mine Sweeper is a game on most computers in which the player is supposed to click on squares in hopes that there will not be a bomb under the square. If successful, the square will reveal nothing or it will reveal a number that tells you how many bombs surround that square. But every once in a while you will click on one tile and about 50 squares will disappear. Why? Because you clicked on an area of the game board that has nothing under it.

THIS IS THE SAME THING that should happen in your marriage conflict resolution. You will go back and work through a single issue and bring it to resolution. Your cloud may not be much lighter after one conflict is resolved. But you just spent 15 to 30 minutes in good, quality, marital communication. And one of these days, you will resolve a problem that looks so much like about 50 other issues you have had that, by agreement, you will erase all 50 of those problems at once. It can happen. But you have to start with one problem. Get it resolved, and go on.

The C*E*A*S*E Fighting model of conflict resolution has five steps based on each of the letters in the word CEASE. But before you begin, there are two major rules the couple must obey. Here they are:

Pre-C*E*A*S*E Rule #1— You must center in on one issue only. Because problems and issues entered your marriage one at a time, they must leave one at a time. And even though women can wrestle with and address multiple issues at once, men cannot. So, for the sake of problem resolution, we must address one issue only.

We will take up the sock-on-the-floor issue that we brought up a couple of chapters ago. I threw a pair of socks at the hamper but only one made it in. I walked away and my wife told me to pick it up. I told her to pick it up. We exchanged unpleasantries until we both left, slamming doors, and not talking to each other for three days. You may be surprised to find out that this was not the first time this happened in our marriage. But even if the same problem happened once before, or many times before, you must address only one incident at a time. So, we agree that we will talk about the sock-on-the-floor incident that happened last Tuesday after we came home from our friend's party. The couple also agrees not to bring up those other incidents as ammunition against each other. It never helps, it never works. Stop it!

Pre-C*E*A*S*E Rule #2— You must make an appointment. To resolve a marriage problem both must be in a problem-resolving mood. What mood? Well, the mood should be one of humility, love, caring, and willing to do anything FOR the other to get the problem resolved. This cannot happen on the spur of the moment. You cannot approach your spouse and say, "We have to talk about this right now!" Ambushing your spouse is not permitted. Also, you cannot effectively resolve a problem if you are still experiencing the heated emotions of the problem. Both must calm down. Those heated emotions will never resolve the problem. Make an appointment that both will agree to. "Honey, maybe we can talk about this tonight at 5:00."

Making appointments with your spouse has several benefits. First, it protects both partners from being ambushed. Second, it allows time for emotions to calm. And third, it compartmentalizes the negatives in the relationship. If you both agree to talk about the issue at 5:00 pm tonight, it frees you to do good and positive things for each other in the meantime. You haven't forgotten about the problem. You haven't swept it under the rug. But you have agreed to delay the negativity and put it into a healthy time frame in which you both can work through the problem to the point of resolution. It's a win/win situation.

Let's review. Before you can work through the five-step C*E*A*S*E Fighting model of conflict resolution, you must (Rule #1) center in on a single issue, and (Rule #2) make an appointment that is convenient for both. Now you're ready for conflict resolution.

Step One– The "C" stands for "Confess"

Since every problem begins with selfishness, every problem resolution must begin with self-less-ness. Both parties must be humble, willing to admit what he/she did wrong that made a small issue blossom into a full-fledged war. So, both will confess to what they did wrong that either caused the problem OR added to the problem.

The husband should always go first. Why? Humility comes easier for the woman than for the man. Yet it is the husband that should be the example for his family. So, go first, even if you are not good at it. You'll get better. Your wife will love the effort.

There is one major rule in this step that must be obeyed: You cannot use the word "you." Too many times an apology containing the word "you" comes across as an accusation. For example, "I'm sorry you got upset." That's not an apology, it's an accusation that your mate got upset or that he/she is one with the problem, not me. Make every attempt to craft your confession whereby the word "you" is not used.

So I search my own heart to see what I did wrong in the sock-on-the-floor incident. I begin: "Honey, I am so sorry because I threw the sock on the floor and I walked away. And I yelled and used hateful name-calling. And I slammed the door and didn't speak for three days. I'm very, very sorry." Wives, resist the urge to make suggestions for more confessions. Let him talk and open his heart to you. And if he did ten things wrong but only confesses to three, that's okay. You both will be able to bring up other things later in this process.

After the husband finishes, the wife goes. If you did not start the problem, don't confess to it. But you did do something to add to the wrongness of the whole fight. So my wife begins: "Honey, I'm so sorry because I snapped and got excited about the hurt I was feeling and said some awful things. I yelled and used hateful name-calling. And I'm very, very sorry." Husbands, don't make suggestions on what else she can confess to. Just appreciate her open heart. Once the wife is finished, you can go to the next step.

Why should you confess to each other? First, confessions settle the mood, disarm and humble both parties. Problems exist when we draw our battle lines and build our walls. Confession removes the barriers. Second, confessions allow for emotional connection. We connect with the heart of our spouse by communication. Healthy, humble communication goes a long way.

Step Two– The "E" stands for "Explain"

Everyone involved in conflict has an overwhelming desire to get their point across. Each wants the other to see their side of the argument. This is a valid need. But what usually happens is that the couple expends a lot of energy foiling any attempt to see or understand the other. There are many weapons couples will pull out like:

- Talking over the other—loudness drowns out the cries of the other
- Invalidation—"Are you kidding me?" "Are you SERIOUS?" "Where in the WORLD did that come from?" "Were you at the same party that I was at?"
- How about this—Irate-ology! This is the idea that anger will explain logic. If your wife is not listening or not getting what you are saying, you might try yelling and saying the same thing again, slowly, as you would to a child. Keep getting louder! I'm sure that if I get more irate she'll start listening.

That stuff doesn't work. But we still have this need to get across what we're feeling. Here's a surefire way to get the point across. It'll be weird, at first, but you'll have fun.

In this step you will explain to your spouse WHY you did what you did. You will say, "I felt_*(give an emotion)*_ like_____*(give an simile)*_____." A simile is a statement or a story with a similar message that explains the reality. For example: "I felt angry, like when Mt. St. Helens was rumbling and quaking for a long time and then finally POW it blew up." So what does this accomplish? I just got through telling my wife that she made me so angry that I was about to blow up. But if I had used those words, it would have reignited the fight. But if both of us are able to look somewhere else, like towards the North, at a volcano rumbling and exploding, I can get across the point that I was very angry, AND my wife can see my emotion and understand a bit of what's going on inside me. Notice the severity of the simile. If I had said, "I felt angry, like I was walking across the living room and stubbed my toe on a pillow," that would indicate that my anger was slight. But if I compared my anger to a mountain exploding, then I have communicated a more severe form of anger.

Using similes helps the couple to temporarily focus on something other than each other. You can use TV shows, movies, books, made-up characters, cartoons, historical figures, etc. But make sure that your simile takes the focus away from the two of you. If you say, "I felt angry, like that last time you…," your focus is too close and you are re-accusing your mate of a past event. Not good.

Have fun creating similes. The more outrageous the simile, the better it will be for conflict resolution.

Back to the problem at hand. I threw a pair of socks at the hamper. One of the socks landed on the floor, and I just walked away. We said many hateful things trying to make the other pick up the sock. We ended up slamming doors and not talking to each other for three days. So, why did I do that? "Well, I felt…cornered, like…when Daffy Duck was painting the floor, and he kept walking backwards until he was stuck in the corner. He tried to turn right, then left. But he couldn't go anywhere. So he cried 'Aaaaaaaaah' because he didn't know what else to do." I like cartoons, can you tell? But I basically told my wife that the way she was talking to me put so much pressure on me and "trapped me into a corner" that I felt like exploding. The simile, watching a cartoon duck, was non-threatening. And my wife, at least for the moment, could see what went on inside of me during that conflict.

Now it's my wife's turn. Why did she yell and scream and slam doors. "Well … I felt … belittled … like … I was asked to go to a dinner party at my best friend's house and when I arrived they put me at the kid's table. No adult would talk to me the whole time." My wife just explained to me that she felt like I treated her like a child with my tirades and demands. But the simile was non-threatening and, at least for a moment, I was able to look inside her heart and feel the hurt that she experienced during our conflict.

The first two steps in this model are designed to settle the emotions and allow the couple to begin connecting on an intimate level. You both have shown love by humbling yourselves. And, you have taken the time to look into the other's heart. You can now accomplish anything. Time to go to step three.

This email came a few minutes ago. Thought you might appreciate it.

Hi, Bob,

    Gene and I actually used your CEASE tool last night. We butchered it horribly in spots and finally gave up on coming up with a simile but we ended up having a lot of fun in the process. Gene said we should have tried this sooner! Hee hee. Thanks.

Step Three– The "A" stands for "Ask"

Now we're going to start repairing the conflict. In this step you are going to ask your mate for some advice on what you could have done differently so that the problem wouldn't have occurred or wouldn't have gotten so out of hand. The fighting blinds us to the needs of the other. We need to take time here to find out what would have helped your mate handle the situation in a much calmer way.

This is the perfect next step. You both have opened your hearts (Step One), confessing wrongs that you did to cause the problem or add to the problem. You both have opened your eyes and ears (Step Two) as the other described the emotional turmoil he/she felt as the conflict was raging. You are connecting in a way that probably hasn't happened in a while. You are humble, loving, and tender. Now, listen as the other gently gives you advice.

You can use the word "you" in this step. But you must also use the word "maybe" in your advice statements. "Maybe" does two things in marital communication. First, it softens the statement. A parent can speak to a child with authority: "Don't do that!" "You shouldn't have done that!" or "You should've just picked up your sock!" But married couples MAY NOT talk to each other as they would a child. The word "maybe" allows you to talk straight to your spouse, but your statements don't come across as demands. "Honey, maybe you could have just picked up your sock."

The second benefit of using the word "maybe" is that it allows your spouse to retain the right to choose. If a parent commanded a child to put his toys away, the child has no choice but must obey (hopefully) without question or discussion. Married couples MAY NOT talk to each other as they would a child. Giving your spouse advice or direction that comes after the word "maybe" allows him/her to choose whether or not to follow this advice. But hopefully, as humble partners intent on resolving the conflict and strengthening, both will consider seriously what the other says.

So, I threw my socks at the hamper and one fell on the floor. It was an accident! But I walked away. She yelled at me. I yelled at her. Well, you know the rest. In Step Three, the husband again goes first. He says, "Honey, what could I have done differently?" The wife says, "Well, maybe you could have just picked up your sock. And, maybe you could have not yelled at me when you seemed to get irritated. And, maybe you could have talked to me during those days that we didn't speak and ask me gently to forgive you, or talk it out or something." The wife goes as long as she needs to gently advise her husband on what she thinks would have been a better scenario.

When the wife is through giving advice, she asks her husband, "Honey, what could I have done differently?" The husband says, "Well, maybe you could have asked me more gently to pick up my sock. And, maybe you could have not called me those awful names."

What do we accomplish in this step? Many times as we argue we cut off our mate from being able to express what they perceived about what went wrong in the argument. We talk over each other or we shut down. We may bring up past events or generalities in hopes of destroying our mates. When this happens, neither is able to vent in a healthy way, and neither is validated. Step Three allows us to gently express our own views on the situation, knowing that my spouse is really listening. If I am the one listening at the time, I am truly looking into my mate's heart and validating his/her reasonings. It, again, is a win/win situation.

What if something goes wrong?

There is always a chance that one or the other may break a rule and start doing things that hinder proper resolution. Rule-breaking includes: yelling, screaming, bringing up other past problems, using "you" in a way that hurts and degrades the other, etc. But even here, couples MAY NOT speak to one another as they would a child. For this reason, the couple should have a prearranged signal that, when employed, will indicate to the other, "I believe you have broken a rule." By agreement, then, the one talking will stop, consider what he/she just said, think of a better way to present it, and then try again.

The signal could be a secret code word like "Rumplestiltskin" or "coaster." "Honey, would you like a coaster for your glass." There may not be glasses on the conflict resolution table, but the mere mention of the word "coaster" is the signal that says, "Let's stop, and try this again."

The signal can also be a saltshaker or some other ordinary table item sitting at the edge of the table. When one believes the other has broken a rule, he/she gently reaches over, grabs the saltshaker, and places it in the center of the table. Again, both agree to stop, think about what just went on, figure out a better way to say what was said, and try again.

If the signal is employed a second time, the one talking now is allowed to ask, "I'm not really sure what I am doing wrong. Would you please tell me?" The other then gently explains how they feel a rule is being broken.

What if things fall apart while working through the C*E*A*S*E Fighting model? You cannot resolve a conflict if negative emotions are present or if one or both are uncooperative. If things start falling apart, stop immediately, and make an appointment to try it again the next day.

Open Forum

The open forum is the space between Step Three—"Ask" and Step Four—"Servant Solution." By the time you have worked through the first three steps you are humble, open, honest, sharing, forgiving, and gentle in advising. When you get to the fourth step, you are done! Well, what if something happened during our fight that hasn't been brought up yet? Your spouse didn't confess to it and/or you forgot to bring it up when you were giving advice. So, you bring it up here in the open forum.

Couples need to make sure that everything that happened during the conflict is brought up, discussed, forgiven, and put away. For example, what if, because I was so angry with my wife for yelling at me, I went to a friend's house and complained about her, and it angered her. That's something that definitely needs to be talked about. The rules in this forum are no different from the first three steps: be humble, talk mostly about yourself, and use "maybe" a lot.

The wife says, "Honey, when you talked to your friends about what happened, well, that really hurt me and I'm not sure what to do about it." The husband, being gentle and humble, says "Yea, that was really stupid of me. Please forgive me."

The husband may say, "Honey, I know I made you angry, but you broke my favorite dragon figurine. I'm not sure if I should be angry about that or just let it go." The wife, being gentle and humble, may say, "Yea, that was really stupid of me. Please forgive me. I'll go see if I can find another one to replace it."

Whatever the other brings up during this open forum, it must be received with the attitude of "let's get this resolved and go on." The open forum can last five minutes or fifty minutes. It depends on how many of those extra things need to be discussed. When you are both satisfied that everything has been talked out, then proceed to the next step.

Step Four– "S" stands for "Servant Solution"

Since all conflict begins with selfishness, they must be resolved with selflessness or servanthood. In the third step both of you had the opportunity to give each other advice on what you thought the other should have done differently so that problem might never have blown up. Now, you will both tell each other what you will do next time so the same thing doesn't happen.

Make sure you keep the third and fourth steps separate. In Step Three you focus on the incident that occurred. In Step Four you focus on how to avoid the same thing in the future.

The husband goes first: "Honey, next time I will ... I will just pick up the sock so we won't have such a ridiculous fight. And next time I won't yell and scream at you. And if it seems that you are not feeling so lovingly towards me, I will knock on the door and ask if we can sit down and talk about things." Then it's the wife's turn: "Honey, next time I will just pick up the sock myself and we won't have this big fight. Or, next time I will ask you more nicely to pick up the sock. And next time, I won't yell and scream at you. And I won't slam doors and call you names. And I won't walk away for three days."

Step Five– The "E" stands for "Erase" and "Enjoy"

Because it is always damaging to bring up old issues, especially ones that have been resolved, to badger each other, the couple must commit to not bring up those past events. The problem here is that we will never forget what happened that day we fought over a sock on the floor and refused to speak to each other for three days. When a similar problem occurs, it will race to the front of our minds. So, we must make a commitment to leave the past in the past.

God takes this fifth step with us all the time. Jeremiah once quoted God, "…I will forgive your iniquity and remember your sins no more" *(Jeremiah 31:34)*. So I'm thinking, "Yea, right. God can't forget!" What is He really saying? "I promise, from this time forward, I will not bring this sin against you. I will never use this past incident to color my attitude towards you. And every time we interact, we will have a clean slate." What a great way to look at each new problem in marriage. Make the commitment!

When erasing this problem from your lives, the husband goes first. His commitment statement is: "Honey, I promise I will not bring up this incident ever again." The wife does the same. It's a small statement, but it means big things.

Does making a statement like this equal forgiveness? Yes. Forgiveness is not a feeling. Forgiveness is not a compromise or any kind of agreement. It is a decision to not hold past wrongs against your mate. Celebrate! You have just spent time humbling yourselves, confessing wrongs, sharing feelings, asking advice, talking out all the aspects of the issue at hand, and describing your changed behavior so this kind of incident won't happen again. Your words, attitudes, and intents have proven to your mate that he or she is valuable, and that none of this present fight will ever get in the way of true love. You have already committed to putting all of this behind you. The statement is "icing on the cake." Good job!

You now have to kiss and make up. This is the "enjoy" part of this step. If you can't kiss, if there is still some ill feelings about this matter, then you haven't successfully completed the C∗E∗A∗S∗E Fighting steps. If this is the case, put all this aside and try it again tomorrow.

But if you can kiss, kiss a lot. And if it leads to other things, that's okay, too. I hear that make-up sex is pretty amazing. Have fun.

* * * * *

Congratulations! You have just erased one problem from the cloud that hangs over your marriage. The cloud may not feel lighter, but you just spent time in healthy communication with your mate. And, it led to resolution of a problem plus a lot of kissing. Now, look forward to doing this again, perhaps even tomorrow. The more you work through these steps the lighter your cloud becomes. The fog is lifting.

C⋆E⋆A⋆S⋆E Fighting

Pre-CEASE Rule #1 – Decide on a single issue or incident to resolve

Pre-CEASE Rule #2 – Set an appointment to resolve

C— Confess

Confess to what you did to either start the problem or add to the problem. Do not use the word "you," talk only of yourself.

E— Explain

Why did you do what you confessed to doing? "I felt _____ *(give an emotion)* _____ like _____ *(give an simile)* _____."

A— Ask

"Honey, what could I have done differently?" Be direct, say what's on your heart, but use the word "maybe" a lot.

(Open Forum)

Talk about anything else that needs to be discussed and forgiven.

S— Servant Solution

"Honey, this is what I will do next time so we don't have this same problem …"

E— Erase & Enjoy

"I promise I will never bring up this incident ever again."

(Kiss and make up. Kiss a lot!)

Finding a S⋆A⋆F⋆E Place to Talk

THE CONFLICT RESOLUTION MODEL in the previous chapter has a unique place in your marriage. Couples should use C⋆E⋆A⋆S⋆E Fighting steps after a problem has blown up. C⋆E⋆A⋆S⋆E Fighting is designed to repair a damaging incident.

But what about important issues that need to be addressed? What about those dangerous subjects, you know, the ones you know will get out of hand once you bring them up? How can we talk about important issues in a way that won't blow up all over us? The S⋆A⋆F⋆E Place is such a tool that can be used so the couple can begin conversations on hot topics.

Marital communication falls apart when conversation changes into argument. Remember this: the moment it changes into argument, you both have lost the attention of the other. Both will then try to out argue, out slander, and out scream the other. This just throws you back into a very dangerous fog. Here's what might happen:

- **Misunderstanding**— Not only do you speak a different language than your mate, you now think that increasing the volume of your argument will somehow magically allow your mate to understand a foreign language.
- **No listening**— Often both sides will be polite enough to allow the other to vent, but only to wait for an opening so they can fire their own arguments back.
- **Build up to an explosion**— The volume of the argument rises, the energy level increases, and the tension between the two becomes unbearable. If you are not careful, you will say and do things that will inflict long-term damage
- **Old problems are brought up**— In our desire to win arguments, we bring up past faults to punish the other. It's as if we are saying, "You don't even have a right to talk to me because of what you did last year…." The present argument is overshadowed by EVERY error from the past.
- **Sarcasm becomes the defense**— "Oh, you should talk …" "That's just brilliant. Why don't we all just go throw ourselves off a cliff …" When we use sarcasm, we communicate, "This is how stupid

your argument is, and by the way, this is how stupid you are …"

- **Name-calling intended to destroy**— Once we get to the name-calling stage, we are through arguing. We label the other as worthless (whatever the particular name we use) and try to go on our merry way.

- **Lasting damage to the relationship, FRUSTRATION** — We are not satisfied with how things went. We are frustrated that we cannot get through to the other. We do not successfully vent. The ill feelings stay inside and eat away at our hearts.

- **Lasting damage to the relationship, RESENTMENT** — Whenever we see the other, anger swells up inside. Whenever we think of the other, anger swells up inside. We start hating ourselves because of the stupidity we displayed by even considering that this person might be a good mate.

- **Lasting damage to the relationship, APATHY**— Hatred is not the worst emotion couples feel towards one another. Apathy, when we get to the point where we don't care any more, is worse. We give up. If we're not careful, this could be the "point of no return" for the marriage.

Jane came to talk to me about an on-going problem that caused a lot of ill-feelings between them. When she married Howard, Jane brought her 16-year-old son into the new step-family. Jane spoke of how Howard and her son, Jim, do not get along. Howard tries to act like Jim's father, but Jim resists this idea and vocally pushes this new father figure away from his life. The relationship is a series of arguments and fights. "He just yells at Jim all the time. It's like he can never do anything right. Howard gets upset at everything he does. I have tried to talk to Howard many times about this, and he gets upset at me. He says I don't respect him or that I don't want him to be

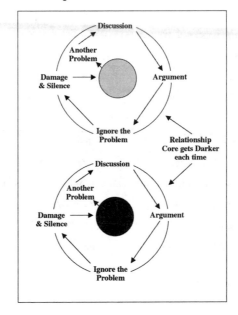

the man of our house. I resigned myself to the fact that we can never talk about this. But it's eating me up inside. I'm at the breaking point. If something doesn't change, I'm going to take my son and leave."

Howard and Jane, like so many couples, get into an argument cycle. It begins with an important matter that must be discussed. The matter turns into an argument. Damage is inflicted on both parties. Then they enter the silence phase in which both ignore the problem and each other. Once the cycle is complete, ill feelings continue to darken the core of the marriage, forever! Stop the madness!

It's time to go to the S*A*F*E Place to talk. The following steps are designed to help you have the right approach and the right attitude to talk about important topics in your marriage. Follow them carefully. Practice them daily. Eventually you will be able to do what you're supposed to do naturally. Let's get started.

Step One– The "S" stands for "Secure Zone"

Your arguments take place in battlefields. Nothing can be resolved there. So we must go to the opposite place. The Secure Zone, by agreement, is a place and time when both parties agree to talk calmly about the issue. Both parties agree that they will talk with the attitude of getting the issue resolved. And, both parties agree that they will come with the attitude of "What can I DO for my partner to help get this resolved?" Both partners must feel safe to vent or describe an awkward or volatile situation.

The first thing that must happen in any conflict is to schedule the meeting. "Honey, do you think that we could sit down at 5:00 pm tonight and talk about this?" Scheduling is important. First, it puts the discussion at a later time when both can cool down. Second, it allows both parties to think about the issue before coming to the table. Now, this is not a time to craft arguments to prove one's side of the case. We are going to the S*A*F*E Place to resolve whatever is hurting the marriage. Third, it allows for compartmentalization of negative issues. We must confront, address, and resolve problems in marriage. But if we schedule the right time to do such, the rest of the time we can spend on building up our marriage with healthy conversation and behaviors. Compartmentalization also limits the time spent on the hot topic. Never spend more than an hour confronting issues. The ideal time would be from 20 to 40 minutes. If it goes past this time, agree to stop and try it again tomorrow.

Step Two– The "A" stands for "Accusation Free"

Arguments fail when they begin to accuse the other rather than offer explanations. If we continue to accuse, we will never get to the point of real communication much less the point of resolution. In this step both partners will agree to design their statements so the other will feel safe enough to truly listen.

The first thing to remember here is that neither is allowed to use the word "you" at first. Too many times statements with "you" come across as accusations. "I'm sorry you got upset." "I was so angry when you came home late without calling me like you were supposed to." Though the couples need to discuss anger and rule-breaking, when statements like these come out the other may feel like he or she is being re-accused of fault. The listening stops and the S⋆A⋆F⋆E Place is no longer safe.

Craft your statements or questions without "you." "Honey, the other night I was so angry, I was so upset, and I know I really blew it. But I didn't know what else to do. What can I do about this?" When discussions begin this way, the mate gets a clear picture of what might be going on inside you. And, because walls of defense are not erected, he/she will be able to join in a discussion.

"Honey, when I was at home at 8:00 the other night, and I was all alone, my mind went crazy as to what was happening. Was I supposed to get mad, was I supposed to worry? I don't know. But what I did was explode. I know that probably wasn't right, but I didn't know what else to do? What can I do?"

Try to end your initial statements with a non-threatening question. In this way you mate will feel like he or she is more there for resolving the matter than being a target for your anger.

This step is also a great place to include similes in your descriptions. Just like in the previous chapter, you can use similes to help your partner see what your emotions look like. Use this formula: I felt_____ *(give an emotion)* _____ like_____ *(give a simile)* _____." "I was so upset the other night, I felt <u>frightened</u> like <u>a little girl waiting at the park, after dark, because her father said he'd be there within an hour, but she waited there all night wondering if her father cared enough to come pick her up.</u>" Similes can be a great way of expressing emotions. But take care that your simile is far enough removed from your situation that your mate does not become offended by your illustration.

Step Three– The "F" stands for "Fair Grounds"

In marital conflict, one of the partners is usually more dominant in conversation and/or demeanor than the other. When this happenes, the weaker one may try to join in the argument, but when he/she feels overwhelmed they will shut down and just take what the other dishes out. This never results in a resolution of the problem. It only extends it, puts it off until the next time tempers flare.

In many arguments, the offended one is more vocal than the guilty party. When arguments begin in this way, the offended may feel certain rights and privileges above the other. "I'm not the one who came home late." "I'm not the one who wrecked the car." While the statements may be true, the attitudes can never help resolve any argument. The one who is in the wrong already knows he/she is in the wrong and probably feels remorse. But if the mate continues the condemnation, the other may shut down not knowing how to handle the abuse. Yes, that's right, abuse. There is no safety here. There is no way to resolve matters this way.

Even if you are the "innocent" party, you must still come to the S*A*F*E Place with humility, with the attitude of "What can I DO for my partner that will help resolve this matter?"

Fair Grounds are where both parties feel equal, both can be heard equally, and both will work hard to resolve the issue. So, be gentle when you speak, humble when you listen, and encouraging when you resolve.

Step Four – The "E" stands for "Emotions in Check"

Even with the best of intentions the healthy discussion may take a wrong turn. What does a wrong turn look like?

- Anger or other strong emotions re-enter the discussion
- One seems to be criticizing or condemning the other rather than simply expressing emotions
- One seems to be raising his/her voice
- Any of the rules of the S*A*F*E Place are broken

Even when rules are apparently broken, neither is allowed to police the other or treat the other like a child. The couple must come up with some kind of signal that, by agreement, means that one believes the other has broken a rule or that one believes the discussion is taking a wrong turn. The signal can be a code word, or it can be an object that is placed in the center of the table. Either way, when the signal is employed the one talking stops, considers what he or she might have said that broke the rules, then tries to communicate again. If the signal is employed a second time, the one talking is then allowed to ask, "Honey, I'm not really sure why you have used the signal. Would you please tell me?" The other then gently and humbly explains why they employed the signal. "Honey, it seems to me that you are raising your voice a little."

Much more can be accomplished when couples communicate humbly and as equals. Be sure that your emotions are in check at all times.

A Variation of the S*A*F*E Place

Men, there are times when our wives need to vent. They may just need to get a painful matter off of the heart. When this is necessary for them, it is very important that you don't interfere with it. You see, when a painful event occurs, it bruises women's hearts. The way to un-bruise the heart is to talk about the pain, not to fix it, but just to get it out. We men may never truly understand this need. It may help if you find a copy of the song "I just want to be mad for a while" by Terri Clark. It might help a little. Here's the chorus:

I'll never leave. I'll never stray. My love for you will never change. But I ain't ready to make up. We'll

*get around to that. I think I'm right. I think you're
wrong. I'll probably give in before long. Please don't
make me smile. I just want to be mad for a while.*

There are times when our wives need to process pain
in their own way. Sometimes they need to just be mad for a
while. Sometimes they need to just vent. On those occasions
when venting is a necessary step in processing a conflict,
couples can use this variation of the S*A*F*E Place.

First, women let your husbands know when you need
a time to just vent. Be clear to them about your intent
because they won't get it on their own. "Honey, I need to
spend some time venting about_____. Would
it be okay if I did all the talking and you just listen?"

Second, make an appointment. Husbands, you should
get to the point where you are willing to drop everything
and listen to your wives the moment they need you. But
wives, even if you are ready to vent, and your husband
may not be in a vent-listening mode, allow him time to
prepare himself. "Honey, would it be OK if we sat down at
5:00 tonight so I can get this off my heart?"

Third, be sure that this venting session doesn't last
more than 30 minutes. It would be better if it were limited
to 15 minutes. Your husband will try his best to listen and
empathize with you. But it will be difficult. Give him a
break. Put a time limit on your venting. If you don't get it

all out, say, "Thanks for listening. I'm not sure I got it all out yet. Can we do this again tomorrow night at 5:00?"

Fourth, when the venting is over, discuss as a couple if anything can be fixed (for the husband's sake) and how it might be resolved. Humbly talk about how each of you can handle future situations like this in healthier ways. When you are done, kiss! Kissing is always good for a married couple.

Another Variation of the S∗A∗F∗E Place

Couples will often have differing opinions about matters from trivial to earth-shattering, from subject like politics to raising children. These kinds of arguments may lead to full-scale battles. Try a variation of the S∗A∗F∗E Place to talk about these matters, especially if you don't know how your partner will react to such topics.

First, set an appointment to talk about a specific matter. "Honey, would you be willing to sit down with me at 5:00 tomorrow night so I can tell you about my feelings on_____?"

Second, ask for uninterrupted time to talk. But make sure it is a set amount of time. You will also offer your mate the same privilege on a different date. "I would like to talk to you about this for about 15 minutes, but I want you to listen and not talk. Would that be okay?" Assure your partner that he or she will have the same opportunity the next night.

Third, obey the rules of the S*A*F*E Place. Even though you will do all the talking and your partner will do all the listening, you must still approach this time with the humble attitude, knowing that you are bringing up something that you are willing to resolve. Be sure to talk about yourself and keep from using "you" in your remarks. You don't want to attack a sitting duck.

Fourth, if you are the one listening the whole time, try your best to tune into the other's words. If you are able, make remarks that show you are truly listening. Don't be fake! But you can say things like, "Really? Wow," "Oh, that's awful," or "Yeah, I know." When your mate is through talking, assure him or her that you want to help in any way to resolve or fix or come to an agreement on whatever subject was brought up.

Fifth, make an appointment for the other partner to be able to share. If you took 15 minutes, allow your partner to take the same amount of time. Be sure that this second round is done at least one day later so it does not come across as retaliation.

* * * * * * * *

The S∗A∗F∗E Place is a great tool to get you started in talking about difficult matters. Use it well and keep your marriage safe!

The S⋆A⋆F⋆E Place

S— Secure Zone

Attitude - humble. Atmosphere - calm. Speech - gentle.

A— Accusation Free

Talk about yourself. Use similies. End with questions, "What should I do?"

F— Fair Grounds

Communicate as equals. Attitude = "What can I DO for him/her to help resolve this matter?"

E— Emotions in Check

Careful! Don't let the situation get out of control. Use a code word to stop escalations.

Making a
Faithfulness Plan

HAVE YOU HEARD THE PROVERB: The one who fails to plan, plans to fail? It's true. If we do not make a plan to stay faithful there is a greater chance we may fall into an affair. Here are some shocking statistics:

- 22 percent of men and 14 percent of women admit to having extramarital affairs
- One researcher estimates that 60 percent of all men and 40 percent of all women will have an extramarital affair sometime in their lives
- One in every 2.7 marriages are affected by affairs
- Most married couples affected by affairs will stay together
- Only 17 percent of divorces in America are because of affairs

Here is my own statistic from my counseling experience: 90 percent of all couples who come to me for counseling have an affair in their past. People are cheating in droves. We see it all the time. Media almost normalizes extramarital affairs unless it makes good business sense to condemn some political figure in public. And, even then, most of those couples choose to stay together.

Unfaithfulness causes enormous damage to marriage. Even if the couple should decide to stay together, they don't often seek the kind of help they need to work through the problem and come to a resolution. They live "unhappily ever after."

Though it seems that "everyone cheats," not everyone cheats. And you can do something positive, pro-active, to make sure you will always be faithful to your mate. Making a faithfulness plan can be one of the most romantic things you can do for each other. It is a document that announces to your mate, and to the world, that you will spend time and energy to remain faithful. It's a great plan.

Be sure that you understand what we are asking you to do. I want you to create a one-page document, with five components, announcing your intentions and activities for remaining faithful. When you are done, this document will be signed and dated as you would any binding contract. Put an official seal on it if you have access to such. Then put it in a frame and hang it on your living room wall for all to see. With that in mind, let's get started.

Component #1 – A Statement of Love

Do you remember the day you stood in front of a minister or judge and announce your love for the one you married? This statement of love is the same kind of statement you made right before you said "I do!" But now it is a statement of recommitment for the love you have for your mate. The reason you are providing this faithfulness plan in the first place is to prove your undying love for him or her. Begin your statement with something like, "Honey, with all my heart, I love you for …" Make it a statement that you would be able to use as you play the leading role in a movie, with orchestra music in the background, stars twinkling in the sky, and the moonlight hitting your eyes just right. It should make your mate melt. Here's one example:

Honey, with all my heart, I love you for choosing me out of all the other possibilities in the world. You are the most wonderful woman in my life. There has never been another and there will never be another.

Corny? No. Beautiful! Saying "I love you" should be a daily part of every marriage. But here, within the framework of this magnificent document of faithfulness, it should be earth-shattering. We forget how powerful words can be. Take this opportunity to open the ears and heart of your mate.

Component #2 – A Statement of Commitment

Making a statement of love should be an easy task. But describing your commitment to make your marriage work for the rest of your life may be a bit more challenging. Don't think about the "rest of your life." Instead, just make a commitment to your mate for the next fifty or sixty years.

You cannot stay faithful accidentally. So, make the statement. Include things like "whatever it takes" or "all my energy" or always and forever." Here's my statement:

Today, I commit my heart, my mind, my soul, and all my strength to you, to stay faithful to you, and to you only, for the rest of my life. I will do whatever it takes to keep myself pure for you, for us, for our marriage, for our family, and for our future.

What man or woman would not want to hear these words? In statements like this one you are not only promising to be faithful, but you are pouring romance all over each other. It's like a gift that keeps on giving.

Component #3 – Faithfulness Steps

Faithfulness does not simply mean an absence of unfaithfulness. There are lots of couples out there that are not unfaithful to each other, but neither are they confident about their mates' intentions. Go beyond a blanket statement that you will be faithful. How will your remain faithful? What steps will you take to assure your mate of your good intentions?

In this section, list steps that you will take. Make anywhere from three to ten statements. Use only positive statements here. In other words, these are positive, proactive things that you will do for your mate. Here are some example statements:

- I will let you know when I will be late coming home from work and why.
- I will not be at the office alone with someone of the opposite sex.
- I will always be honest about whom I am with
- I will introduce you to all of my friends and not have any friends that you do not know about.
- My cell phone and email will always be available to you if you ever want to see with whom I communicate.
- I will speak only good things about you to my friends and co-workers.

If you have been having trouble in the past with certain issues, put some statement of faithfulness that will soothe your mate's stress about you. For example, if there has been an issue about giving a ride home to a co-worker of the opposite sex, write something like, "I will not be alone in a car with a co-worker of the opposite sex." This kind of promise will force you to make sure someone else is riding with you when you take that particular co-worker home. But these things are worth the effort if they will reassure your mate of your faithfulness.

Component #4 – My Plans for When Something Goes Wrong

Even with the best of intentions, things happen that put us into situations that we try to avoid. So what do we do then? If you happen to find yourself alone at night at your workplace with a co-worker of the opposite sex, and you don't tell your mate for fear they will not trust you, but later he or she finds out, how much trouble will you be in? Things happen. But prepare yourself on what you will do if you find yourself in a situation you are trying to avoid.

In this section of your faithfulness plan, tell your mate what steps you will take once you find yourself in the wrong place at the wrong time. If you tell your mate in advance, AND do what you said you would do, your mate will trust you.

Let me illustrate how effective this section can be in your own marriage. I have a faithfulness plan in my counseling practice. First, I do not counsel with a woman in my office when there is no one at the reception desk. But even then, after I go into my office with my client and shut the door (this is necessary for confidentiality), is there a possibility the woman client may cross the line and proposition me? Yes, the possibility is real. Even if a live person is sitting at the reception desk, just 20 feet from where my client and I are sitting, it may not deter her from crossing the line, so we start working the plan. Second, the one at the reception desk knows my faithfulness plan and is ready to act. Third, we work the plan. Here it is:

- I stop everything, get up, and invite the one sitting at the reception desk to come into my office with my client and I, as a witness.
- I then tell my client, "You have crossed the line, and I will no longer counsel with you. If you need me to refer you to someone else, I will. But know this, I am going to leave my office and find my wife and tell her what happened here today. And, apart from me, you, my wife, and my receptionist, no one will hear about this incident. Now, please leave my office."
- Then I go find my wife and explain to her what happened.

Is there a possibility the female client will go out and lie about the situation and say that I made a pass at her and get me in trouble? Yes, there is that possibility. But what do you think would be better, for me to tell my wife what happened as soon as it happened, or to wait for a couple of weeks or a couple of months for the rumors to trickle back to her and then try to explain to her that I was innocent? Whether the lie from the female client gets me in trouble or not, the only one I really care about in that situation is my wife. And she will know, because we made the plan and worked the plan, that what I said is the truth.

Here are some statements you can put into this component of your faithfulness plan. Be sure to cover things that have happened in the past that caused trouble between you and your mate.

- I will walk away from my buddies when they start telling sexual jokes.
- If my ex-girlfriend calls or emails, I will not respond and I will call and tell you immediately what has happened.
- If a co-worker of the opposite sex wants me to stay late and work alone with him or her, I will respectfully decline, even if it means I will miss out on overtime.
- If a co-worker of the opposite sex asks me out for drinks after work, I will either say, "No thanks" or

"Sure, my wife and I would love to come out for drinks."

If you find yourself working one of these plans, be sure to contact your mate immediately and let him/her know what happened.

Component #5 – A Statement of Faith in My Marriage

The reason you are creating this faithfulness plan is to protect you, your mate, and your marriage. Why? What's so special about marriage that you will go to such lengths to ensure its survival? That's what you need to tell your mate. As you finish this document, tell your mate how special marriage is to you. Here's an example:

Honey, there is nothing more important to me than you. I want our marriage to last so we can grow old together. I promise to be the husband you need and to honor the vows I made with you 33 years ago. I love you.

What a beautiful "I do" statement that will help you recommit your life to your mate.

Before you Create the Document

The whole purpose of creating a faithfulness plan is to assure your mate of your love and faithfulness. I want you to search your own heart and come up with assurances. But consider what your mate might want to see in your plan.

At the end of this chapter is a work sheet labeled "Before you write your plan." As a couple you need to sit down and ask, "What would you like to see in my faithfulness plan?" You might find out that your mate has a concern that you were not aware of.

Mary and Barry sat down to work on this exercise one night. Mary confessed to her husband that she felt uncomfortable when he went to the bank. To her it seemed as if he always went when he knew a certain teller would be there and wait for her to wait on him. Mary went to the bank with Barry one day and saw him flirting with the teller. Barry didn't feel he was flirting. But it didn't matter. If his wife had a problem with that teller, he would make a plan that would assure his wife of his faithfulness. When it came time to present his plan to his wife, Barry had included these words, "I will no longer use the 117th Ave branch to make my deposits. I will use the one on Hickory St. And, anytime you want to go with me to the bank, I will be honored."

Make an appointment with your mate to go through the worksheet. Set aside a half hour to an hour of uninterrupted time. Don't tell each other what to write. Gently let your mate know what would help you feel more secure. Once you have this information, go off and write out your faithfulness plan.

Create the Document

Use your imagination when it comes to creating the Faithfulness Plan document. It can look like a diploma or marriage certificate. Word and Publisher software can help you design something for your own tastes. You can, as some couples have done, write out the plan by hand. One woman cut a heart-shaped card out of construction paper and wrote her plan around all the curves of the heart. Whatever you want to do, do it. Then, when you're ready, set up a special time to present it to one another. Before you give it to your mate, read it to him or her. You'll feel closer than you have felt in a long time.

At the end of this chapter there is a Faithfulness Plan template so you can see all five components that should be included. You may copy the template exactly or revise it to fit your needs.

Also included at the end of this chapter are actual faithfulness plans from one couple who had gone through one of my marriage workshops. They were so excited about the faithfulness plan that they went home to work on it immediately after the workshop.

Focus your mind on your mate. It's he or she that you want to impress. Give assurances, grant love, and build confidence.

Before you write your plan...

The faithfulness plan is your gift to your mate. It needs to come from your heart. But it is supposed to touch your mate's heart. So, even though your mate shouldn't tell you what to write, you should know what's important to your mate. The following exercise gives you both an opportunity to suggest what would be important to you as you read your mate's faithfulness plan. So, spend some time offering suggestions to each other. Example: "I would like to see something about not talking about my sister" or "I would like to see something about not comparing me to your ex."

FOR THE HUSBAND, WHAT WOULD YOU LIKE TO SEE IN YOUR WIFE'S FAITHFULNESS PLAN?

1. _____

2. _____

3. _____

4. _____

5. _____

6. _____

FOR THE WIFE, WHAT WOULD YOU LIKE TO SEE IN YOUR HUSBAND'S FAITHFULNESS PLAN?

1. _____

2. _____

3. _____

4. _____

5. _____

6. _____

Template—

My Commitment to Be Faithful

My love, with all my heart …

Today, I commit to you my heart, my soul …

To show my commitment to you, I will:

1. Always tell you if I will be late …

2. Introduce you to all my friends …

3.

4.

5.

If something should go wrong, I will:

1. Call you immediately and tell you what happened

2. Show you all the emails I get from my ex

3.

5.

There is nothing more important to me in life than you.
I want our marriage to last until …

_____ _____

   Signed   *Date*

Sample "Faithfulness Plan"

My Faithfulness Plan to My Husband

MY GREATEST LOVE, the love of my life: I love you more than words can express for sacrificing so much to be with me. Thank you for loving me, faults and all. You are the only man I'll ever need, the only man I want.

Today and always, I give you my whole heart, mind, body and soul. These are yours and yours alone to nurture, to comfort, to accept, and to love. I'm willing to do whatever it takes to protect the sanctity of our marriage. I'm committed to only you until my days on earth are through.

I promise to practice the following plan:
- I will always let you know if I am running late and why.
- I will always be honest about where I am and who I am with.
- I will introduce you to all my friends, and not keep friends you don't know about.
- I will never do anything alone with anyone of the opposite sex.
- My cell phone and email will always be available to you.
- I will always speak only good things about you to my friends, family, and coworkers.
- I will keep all communication with members of the opposite sex in a public forum (i.e. MySpace, Facebook).
- If I ever feel the need to seek something I am lacking, I will seek it from you and only you.
- I will ALWAYS tell you the truth, maintaining complete honesty and transparency.

Should any uneasy situations arise, I promise to follow this plan:
- If any exes call, text, or email, I will not respond and let you know immediately.
- If someone of the opposite sex asks me to do something with him, I will respectfully decline or make sure you are welcome also.
- If anyone pursues me knowing I'm married, I will immediately cease all contact with that person and tell you what happened.

Every day for the rest of my life, this marriage is my top priority. I will give every ounce of strength and energy to make sure you are confident that I would never stray, and will remain hopelessly devoted to you. I promise to be everything you need and more, and will proudly honor the vows I made on our wedding day. I love you Jon!

_____   _____
Lacey   Date
Your Loving Wife Forever

SAMPLE "FAITHFULNESS PLAN"
MY FAITHFULNESS PLAN TO MY WIFE

MY LOVE, MY STRENGTH, MY WIFE. I truly love you in every way
possible, and I am thankful you are in my life. I have never known
a love so true and will never know a love as true.

Today and for the rest of my life I make this commitment; from my heart and
soul, my body and mind, that I am yours for all of eternity.

My Plans for Faithfulness…

I will let you know where I am and what I'm doing while out and away from
you.
I will always be honest about who I am with.
I will introduce you to all of my friends that you don't know or know about.
My cell phone and emails will always be available should you
ever want to see them.
I will speak only good things about you to my friendsand co-workers.

If Uneasy Situations Arise…

If an ex-girlfriend emails me, I will not respond.
And I will be honest and tell you right away.
If a member of the opposite sex makes a pass at me or is interested in being
anything more than friends I will announce to them that I'm taken! Married
to the most beautiful woman God ever created!

My Love, my Strength, my Wife…

I will put nothing before you or our relationship again. I want to live out
our dreams together in a marriage that will last and grow stronger than ever
imagined. I promise to be the husband you need and deserve, I promise to
honor my vows until death do us part.
I love you Lacey … with all that I am. —Jon

_____   _____

Jon   Date

Note: In a letter that accompanied these Faithfulness Plans, Lacey said:
   *One month ago, Jon and I were ready to be done, to the point he moved out and I
hired a lawyer. I wanted to send you mine and Jon's Faithfulness Plans. We sorta did
our homework out of order. Given our specific situation, we felt there was a greater
priority to get the Faithfulness plans done right away. We both had a great time doing
it, and I know to me, it felt really good to hear those promises from him.*

What if I'm the Only One Wanting to Make My Marriage Work?

IT'S ALL MATHEMATICAL. It's all about the numbers. Let's say that both the husband and wife are willing to give a 100 percent effort to make their marriage beautiful and fantastic. Well, mathematically, 100 plus 100 equals 200. So, you have a 200 percent marriage. (Trust me, this is what happens.)

Let's say, one morning the wife wakes up and she isn't so happy to be married so she only gives a 40 percent effort. Well, if the husband gives his 100 percent effort in spite of what his wife does, the couple still has a 140 percent marriage! The same is true if the husband gives only 40 percent when the wife gives 100 percent. Numbers don't lie!

So, you get through reading this fantastic book and soon find that your spouse just doesn't want to work so hard at making your marriage work. First, shame on your spouse! However, if you are willing to work, you can have a good marriage even if your spouse only gives 20 percent or so. See how it works?

Now, I realize that my mathematics may not follow standard mathematical principles, but in marriage this works! In this chapter you will discover ideas and tools that you can use to make your marriage better even if you believe you're the only one working on it. These principles work. Try them. Commit to them. And enjoy the ride.

Here are some Things to Avoid

So you're ready to start working on your marriage by yourself. It will work. Trust me! But make sure you do it the right way. You must have the proper attitude and proper behaviors for all this to go right.

#1— The 50/50 marriage will not work. We did the math for you. The 100/100 marriage will cover the times one or both partners are unwilling or unable to put into the marriage as much as they should. If you should opt for the 50/50 marriage instead, you have already been defeated.

- The 50/50 marriage limits the love you are willing to give. You decide that you will only love up to a certain point, to the same amount of love your mate is willing to give. So, you never give more than half your love, and most of the time it's a whole lot less.

- The 50/50 marriage does not work at all if one or both partners has the slightest hint of insecurity or unhappiness. Once I decide to back away from my full 50 percent, I have already created division in my marriage. "A house divided against itself cannot stand!"

- The 50/50 marriage produces a marriage gap. Call it anything you want. It's ugly. The love gap, the communication gap, the intimacy gap, the trust gap. And, if we are not moving towards our mates, closer to our mates, we are drifting apart.

#2— Waiting for your mate to go first won't work. Every problem or conflict begins with selfishness. I want this, I need this, I demand this. So if you wait, you are showing further selfishness. "I won't do _____ if he won't do _____."

Remember the first "Home Alone" movie? The old man that lived next to Kevin had a fight with his son years earlier and neither wanted to be the first to say "I'm sorry." The old man had to see his granddaughter at the Christmas Mass rehearsal because he couldn't attend mass with his own son. Kevin said something like, "No offense, sir, but it seems kind of silly." Kevin, the 7-year-old kid got the old man to consider making the first move and contact his son. As the movie ends, we see the son, the daughter-in-law, and the granddaughter having a great reunion at the old man's house on Christmas morning.

You don't want to make the first move to help your marriage get stronger? Seems kind of silly.

#3— Bargaining for positions won't work. Negotiating is another way of saying it. But it's really just a roundabout way of controlling the other. Not good in marriage!

All bargaining begins with, "Here's what I want …" What's wrong with this picture already? It is the epitome of selfishness. Bargaining works only for the one who is the best at being selfish.

If I bargain, and agree to serve my mate based on an agreement or expectation of something to be received, I have painted a picture of contractual law, not marriage. There's something drastically wrong with a marriage based on legalese.

If I bargain for positions then any activity that takes place under this kind of agreement has "obligation" as its motive. This is not love. This is not marriage.

#4— Badgering your mate won't work. Though we don't like it we may slip into a position in which our anger will control our thoughts and our words. Instead of healthy communication that will help your mate come closer to your heart, you may lash out in tirades and lectures on how he or she is not doing what is right and how you deserve better. First, what you say during your tirade or lecture is usually right. But the way you say it, intertwined with anger, insults, insinuations, and punishments, will not accomplish what you want to accomplish. Badgering puts you above your mate, looking down on his or her stupidity and failings. Not a good picture for a loving, healthy marriage.

Being the only one in your marriage willing to work and do what is right will be frustrating at times. But, work the plan. Don't resort to badgering. That may just push your mate further away.

The 90 Percent Rules

The ideas, messages, practical hints, and tools in this book are proven aids in helping couples build healthy, happy, loving, and lasting marriages. When couples take the time to communicate, intimacy is built. The sky is the limit for what a couple can accomplish when they work together on their marriage.

But the common problem in marriage repair arises almost 90 percent of the time. The common problem is that usually only one of the partners wants to work on the marriage while the other is either satisfied with the marriage the way it is or has become too apathetic about the marriage to care. Almost 90% of the time the wife is the one who wants to work to improve the marriage.

And, since almost 90 percent of all books are purchased by women, if you are reading this book before your mate does, there is a 90 percent chance that you are a woman seeking ways to improve your marriage. There is also a 90 percent chance you have read other marriage books and have become frustrated when you tried to get your mate to read or practice some healthy marriage lifestyle. Women, guys feel the same way; they just don't talk about it. But you can change your marriage by changing your attitudes and behaviors.

Men, this final chapter, when applied, will out-do any effort your wife might expend for your marriage. When a woman works on her marriage she might be lifted up as a beautiful angel of hope. But when you work on your marriage, you will be lifted up as the knight in shining armor, coming to rescue and protect. There is nothing more beautiful in this world than a powerful man who humbles himself before the queen of his life.

Can you have a better marriage even if you are the only one who is willing to start doing what needs to be done? Absolutely! The blessings and benefits of working on your marriage are not totally dependent on your mate's behavior. It can work.

A woman goes to her lawyer to file divorce papers. "I'm fed up with him. He is uncaring, unloving. He never talks to me. He buries his head in the newspaper or goes into the computer room and stays there until bedtime. And when he talks to me, he doesn't talk. He yells at me. I wish I had never married him. I want a divorce! I want him to suffer for what he did to me and to our marriage." As the woman and her lawyer spoke, they came up with a plan to mentally and emotionally destroy the husband. "Here's what you do," the lawyer said. "Go home, and for the next three months do everything you can for your husband. Rub his back, rub his feet, bring his dinner to him, be an animal in bed. Take care of his every need. Then, when he feels safe and secure in the marriage, POW, we will file the divorce papers and pull the rug out from under him. It will destroy him!" The woman goes home and for the next three months puts all her energies into making sure her husband had everything he needed or wanted. At the end of the three months, the lawyer called the woman and said, "It's time. Come to my office and sign these papers and we'll destroy that sack of garbage you're married to." But the woman objected, "Why would I ever divorce this man? He is the most wonderful husband anyone could ever have."

Your marriage can mirror this story. When we put our efforts into making our mate happy, even if they don't deserve it, several things happen:

- We stop worrying so much about our mate's faults.
- We start expending positive energy that dramatically increases our physical and emotional health.

- We begin to enjoy the benefits that always follow acts of love.

It's a win/win situation. It would be even better if your mate put the same amount of energy into it. But for now, don't worry about that. Just do it. You'll find that your mate becomes more beautiful every day you decide to serve.

A Balanced Approach

Whatever time you have available to set aside to work on your marriage, be sure to have about a 90/10 ratio between taking care of your mate's needs and talking about "hot button" topics. In general, this means spend 90 percent of your time in positive marriage-building interaction, and spend 10 percent of your time wrestling with or resolving conflicts. Take a quick survey of how many hours you interact each day as a married couple. You both go to work, have dinner, and possibly have other evening obligations. So, how much time, each day, can you set aside to proactively work to improve your marriage? Let's say you have one and a half hours every day. This is good, for now, but I hope it will increase in the future. This is the time frame that you need to target every day.

The whole idea of servanthood is to figure out what your mate either needs or wants and serve those needs to the best of your ability. Remember the Mother Teresa Effect? Even if the one receiving your acts of service does not deserve what you will give or cannot or will not reciprocate, you will still feel an enormous sense of well-being that is built into every act. That's the satisfaction of true love.

Be sure that what you do for your mate is in conjunction with your mate's love language (see Gary Chapman, *The Five Love Languages*, Chicago: Northfield Publishing, 2004). For example if your mate enjoys receiving acts of service, then do stuff for him/her. If your mate's love language is quality time, spend time sitting and listening to him or her tell about current events or hopes and dreams. The other three love languages are receiving gifts, words of affirmation, and physical touch. Be sensitive to what he or she truly wants or needs.

Don't try to tackle tough issues every day of the week. One evening every week would be a good plan at first to approach your mate to discuss and resolve conflict. Try to keep your positive interaction and negative interaction at a 90/10 ratio. Your mate will be less defensive about the problem issues if he or she notices a change in your behavior and attitude. If at first your mate is still leery, or even says to you, "Oh, now I know why you've been so nice, you want to attack me now," don't take it as a failure. Just say something like, "No, I'm being nice to you because

I love you. Talking about problem issues is a separate issue. If you're not ready to talk right now, that's okay. Maybe we can talk next week sometime." Then go back to the servant mode.

When you approach your mate to discuss problem issues, approach with a gentle request. "Honey, do you think maybe we could talk about _____ for a few minutes?" An even better request is for a time in the near future that will allow him or her to be more prepared. "Honey, do you think maybe we could talk tomorrow night at 5:00 pm about _____ ?"

Whatever happens, keep up your acts of service. They will help your mate see your sincerity and feel comfortable about talking to you once again.

Servanthood vs. Slavery

Some will object to the idea of serving without receiving anything in return. Here are some complaints I've heard:

"I tried to be a servant, but he just walks all over me."

"I don't want to do what he wants me to do. It's disgusting."

"I try to serve, but she doesn't notice. She doesn't do anything for me."

"It won't work. The more I serve the more he expects me to do. There are not enough hours in the day to take care of him."

All of these statements point to a lack of understanding of servanthood versus slavery. Here are my definitions of both words:

Slavery: absolute helplessness. One person "owns" the other. The slave cannot think for himself or herself. Must obey, ignoring what is right, proper, or disgusting. Abusive, controlling, unfulfilling. Against the law in America.

Servanthood: choice! A servant gets to choose what to do, when to do it, how to do it, how often to do it, and the intensity of what is done. The servant refuses to be a slave and does not jump at the other's demands. If the servant is too tired, he or she doesn't have to do anything. It's always a choice.

Use the following questions to gauge whether your act of service is servanthood, slavery, or just part of your daily routine.

1. Did you get to choose what you did for your mate? If yes—servanthood. If no—slavery. If it was just what you do for him or her every day anyway—routine.

2. Did you enjoy doing it? This is a trick question. You don't have to enjoy the act of service. You just do it because you know your mate will enjoy it.

3. Was what you attempted disgusting or uncomfortable for you? A servant is in control of his or her behavior at all times. If you don't want to do it, don't do it.

4. Did you do it with hopes or expectations that your mate would respond with appreciation or with an act of kindness? If you had any expectations at all, the act was not true servanthood.

5. Did you do it as part of a normal routine in your marriage? If so, it is routine. It could be servanthood. But this would require special emphasis to do so for no other reason than to make your mate happy. So, did you go out of your way to do something that you know your mate either needed or wanted?

Be careful in this area. Spend a lot of energy in being a servant to your mate. But don't waste one second being a slave.

How long will this take?

I told you my story in the first part of this book. My own marriage had gotten to the point in which it wasn't much fun. It wasn't healthy. And, though I could help other couples get back on track towards a healthy and growing marriage, I would go home and enjoy a mediocre existence. Until that one day, when I had an epiphany. I told myself, "I should probably do in my marriage what I tell other couples to do." I decided to be servant to my wife. I stopped dwelling on the things that drove me crazy, upset me, or made me angry. I made a conscious decision to serve, not expecting anything in return.

I remember it took about one year, twelve months, for me. One day I woke up and realized that I had the most wonderful and beautiful wife ever. Then I tried to analyze how it all happened. I remembered that my wife hadn't changed much in that year. But I did realize that I drastically changed my attitude and my behaviors towards my wife. It worked! I began to serve her, not expecting anything in return, and it worked! I am now a happy servant in my thirty-fourth year of marriage.

Will it take a year for you? Maybe, maybe not. For me, it took a whole year to notice the change. But I looked back on that year and saw many times that we were much better off.

So, just get started and don't worry about how long it will take. You will find good changes immediately, mostly within yourself. And the more you serve, the better you will feel about yourself and your mate.

The 60-Day Challenge

I hereby issue you a 60-day challenge to be a servant in your marriage, even if your mate does not do the same. This challenge is designed to jump-start your efforts towards a healthy marriage and to get you on the right track to do so.

The First 30 Days.

- **TNT—Two Nice Things.** You need to find two things you can do for your mate, every week, for no other reason than to make your mate happy. These can be things you know your mate either needs or wants. These two acts of service need to be things that you don't normally do. They should be out of the ordinary, out of the blue, things that might surprise him or her (in a good way). These are pure acts of service. You don't have to enjoy them. Just do them.

- **Put off bad habits/put on good habits.** It takes about 30 days to stop old, bad habits and start new, good habits. Be aware of how you interact with your mate in problem situations. Take a piece of paper and make three columns. In the first column write down a situation that usually becomes a problem in your marriage. In the second column write down how you usually handled the situation. In the third column write down a way how you, as a servant, might handle the situation differently. You can sit and write down many situations at once, or wait and write on your paper as the situations arise. Think of good and healthy ways to serve, again, even if your mate doesn't deserve your kindness.

The Problem Situation	What I usually do
He leaves a glass on the end-table and doesn't take it to the kitchen when he's through.	Get mad, yell sometimes, sometimes try to guilt him into taking his glass to the kitchen.
I do something stupid and she just sits on the couch for the rest of the night not talking to me.	I usually go to the computer room and surf all night until I'm tired.
He wants to leave a party at my friend's house and I want to stay. He goes off and sulks.	I ignore him, make excuses for him like, "Oh, he's just tired," or "Oh, he's just being a jerk. Ignore him."

	What a servant would do I will ask him nicely. Then, maybe I'll just do it. "I'll take care of that, Honey." Then give him a kiss.
	Maybe I'll walk up behind her and start rubbing her shoulders, say, "I'm sorry for what I did." Then, just keep rubbing for a while.
	I can take him aside so we can talk privately. Ask him how badly he wants to leave. Maybe I'll ask if we can stay for just a little while longer. Agree on a time to leave. Then leave at the agreed upon time.

NEVER let your mate see this worksheet. You may be tempted to use it to show off how much you are doing and how little your mate is doing for the marriage. Don't do this. Keep this worksheet a secret.

The Second 30 Days

- Now that you have practiced alternative ways of handling difficult situations, spend the next 30 days of this challenge by adding more and more acts of service for your mate. Keep pushing yourself. When the 60-day challenge is over, serving your mate should come naturally to you. Remember, you are doing this for the sole purpose of making your mate happy and not expecting anything in return. You will find that you are happier and healthier. And, you will notice that your mate is becoming less irritating. It's a win/win situation.

What Legacy Will You Leave Your Children?

THE SUCCESS OR FAILURE OF YOUR OWN MARRIAGE depends on how hard you work. How about a little motivation? Your children are watching. Your grandchildren are watching. And they are creating an expectation and an outlook for their own marriages based on what they see in you. This is the same phenomenon that influences their decisions on whom to marry. Boys usually marry someone a lot like their mothers and girls usually marry someone a lot like their fathers. It's all about proximity and influence. Your children, as they grew or grow up, are constantly being influenced by your marriage. They are in your home. They are forced to watch marriage happen. Good or bad, they become comfortable with your marriage. It becomes normal, at least to them. Then, when they leave home and find a marriage partner, they will work to have a marriage like the one modeled in front of them. That's a heavy responsibility for you.

So, what will your legacy look like? Will it be a positive experience that will influence generations to come, or will it be a negative experience that could wreak havoc through the generations? Consider what Dr. Tim Clinton wrote in his book *Before a Bad Goodbye* (Nashville TN: Word Publishing, 1999, p. 44-45):

> *"Only five out of a hundred spouses interviewed in a major marital study desired a marriage like their parents'. Just five. Why? There were a number of reasons given, but I ultimately believe it's because your kids are watching. You may think you're hiding the anguish produced by your inability to connect and love, but you're kidding yourself. They hear it in every word to each other and see it in your lack of contact. It charges the air. Believe me, you cannot not communicate.*
>
> *"Your words and actions are powerful—and your children observe and interpret them, often accurately. They know, because of the way you feel about each other, that their world is vulnerable and might crumble at any moment. This sense of temporariness can create in them the same level of distress and pain that you are going through— maybe even more. And they're far less prepared to deal with it. So, they'll be dealing with it for a very long time."*

Later experiences influence legacies

A legacy is whatever you leave your children. It is mostly based on what happens last. Though your children will remember things that happened all throughout your marriage, the last events will often color all the others.

For example, a couple with a great marriage most of their lives can give their children amazing, positive memories that will help them have great marriages of their own. But what if this same couple divorces after 30 years of marriage? The children try to make sense of what the parents did. Ugly stories of anger, distrust, and absence of love spew out with hate-filled speech. Those last events will now darken the good times that happened early in the marriage. The couple will leave a legacy of broken promises and broken love.

The opposite can also be true. A couple with a rocky marriage will give their children negative memories on which they will build their own marriages. But what if, after the kids grow up and leave home, the couple decides to make their marriage work? They turn everything around. Forgiveness, trust, and love fill their lives. They travel to see each of their children to explain the change and ask forgiveness for the negative memories they instilled in their children. This couple will leave a legacy of mended relationships and reclaimed love.

Your children are watching you, right now, today! No matter what state your marriage is in currently, you can, you must work on leaving a positive legacy to your children and all those little ones that come after them.

<u>Re-designing your legacy</u>

The best thing that any couple can do for their children to is have a great marriage. It will give them security, hope, and a great outlook for their own marriage. As you work on your legacy, by working on your marriage, consider these Legacy Markers as a gift to your children.

Legacy Marker #1—
The General Marriage Model

The general marriage model has to do mostly with the quantity of years of your marriage. Stay together! This way your children have a model of what marriage is supposed to look like at each anniversary.

Should you divorce, your children will have that model thrust into their lives as well. Statistically, children of divorced parents are more likely than other children to experience divorce in their own marriages. According to researcher Nicholas H. Wolfinger (*Understanding the Divorce Cycle: The Children of Divorce in Their Own Marriages*, Cambridge University Press, 2005) couples are almost twice as likely to divorce if one of them grows up with divorced parents. If both partners grow up with divorced parents, they are three times as likely to divorce. The models of marriage and divorce are very powerful influences on children.

Bill and Jane came in for counseling because of what they said were suspicions and trust issues. This couple had been married for almost ten years. Their third child just entered kindergarten. Bill was an insurance salesman. Jane, a stay-at-home mom up to that point, had never worked outside of the home. She found a job as a secretary for the church they were attending. She poured herself into the job to prove she was a good worker. And she was. Bill thought that Jane was spending too much time and energy on her job and not enough time on her family and her marriage. She would leave work early enough to pick up the kids from school, but would spend a lot of time during the remainder of the day on the phone handling job-related matters. "She doesn't seem to care about us any more." Jane responded with, "I think Bill is having an affair. And if it's not a full-blown affair, he's getting close." As we proceeded I found that Jane's suspicions were not founded on real facts, but on suspicions.

Eventually, I asked Bill and Jane about previous marriages, of which there were none, and their parent's marriages. Bill's parents were still together after 40 years. Jane's parents had divorced after 10 years of marriage. I asked Jane if she could remember why they had divorced. She said, "My dad was an insurance salesman and traveled often. He had women in almost every city. My mom pretended it wasn't happening. When my dad finally left, my mom had no money and no job. It was the worst time of our lives. I'm not going to let that happen to me and my children." As we proceeded in counseling we found that Jane was having episodes of panic based on the model of marriage her parents provided. Up to that time her own marriage mirrored that of her parents. And her parents had provided no model of what marriage was supposed to look like after 10 years.

In counseling, Bill and Jane were taught how to sit down and share deep concerns, work through issues, and resolve small conflicts as they arose. Turning their attention back into their own marriage and not worrying about her parents' marriage helped bring the couple back together. They are still together, celebrating 25 years of marriage. What a great model for their children.

In my own life I am grateful for my own parents who have modeled marriage in front of me. This year in June, Bob & Beverly Whiddon will celebrate 57 years of marriage. My parents have gone through the normal ups and downs in marriage. But they have stayed together no matter what came their way. This is my model of marriage.

My wife's parents have also provided for us a wonderful model of marriage. Through their own ups and downs, John & Mildred Haney will celebrate 56 years of marriage this July.

Your children need a model of what marriage looks like after 10, 20 and 30 years. They need to see what marriage looks like after their own children grow up and leave home. Stay together! Your children will be blessed.

Legacy Marker #2 – The Healthy Marriage Model

Having a long-lasting marriage naturally influences those around you. The general feeling is either, "I wish I had a marriage like them" or "Well, if they can do it, anyone can!" But your children need more than just time. They need to see a healthy marriage in action. Model this in front of them. Make them see what marriage is all about, how wonderful it can be, and how healthy marriages continue to grow as the years pass.

The first thing you need to do is to go back to chapter 4 in this book and review the information on what a healthy marriage looks like. Use this information like a check list, checking it off only when you find or instill these healthy traits in your own marriage.

There are four major things that should be mandatory for all married couples to do, practice, or perform in front of their children. Consider the following:

Practice Conflict Resolution. Every married couple

has arguments. It's a fact of life that when two human beings get together in some kind of marriage, friendship, or other relationship, eventually they will get on each other's nerves. The children know this happens. They cringe when it happens. But do they ever get to see their parents resolve conflicts in healthy ways? Your fighting negatively influences them. But you can negate the negatives by saturating your family with positive marriage behaviors.

Children do not need to be a witness to your discussions over sensitive issues. Be sure that marital conflict resolution takes place in a private arena. But if the kids were there when the conflict arose and blew up, be sure to go to your kids afterwards and let them know you resolved the problem. Say something age-appropriate like, "Mommy and Daddy were mad at each other last night. We're sorry you had to see us like that. But we went and talked and fixed the problem. And now we're not mad any more." Let your children see you as humble, loving parents who are willing to resolve conflicts as they arise. You may even find that your kids will encourage you when you argue: "Mom, Dad, you need to go to the back room and fix your argument." The willingness to resolve conflicts will influence your children as they marry and have conflicts of their own.

Practice Honor. My definition of honor is how a husband and wife treat each other in public. Couples should lift up and brag about their partners. Do this for the sake of your children. Tell them how wonderful their mother or father is. When the child says something like, "Mom's mad at me and she won't let me go outside," you should say, "Your mother loves you very much. She has a good reason she won't let you go outside." Or, about the father who grounds the teen from a questionable party, say, "Your father is a very smart man. When you stop being angry, why don't you go and see if you can talk to him about the reason he won't let you go to that party."

Never let your children say negative things about your spouse. Always go to your mate's defense. Display a united front with any decision that affects the children. Don't let your kids play one of you against the other. "You won't let me go outside because DAD doesn't want me to go!" Your reply: "Oh, no, WE decided, your father and I decided that we don't want you to go outside."

Practice honor in your home. Your children will pick this up and be better off. They will treat their mates like they see you treat one another.

Practice Servanthood. Everything about marriage equates with servanthood. Marriage was the model of interactive relationships that God gave to the world before any other institution. In fact, marriage is the model for salvation. Why? That's the question. Why did God send his Son to die so we could live? Because we are His bride.

It's all throughout the Bible. The great God and husband is seen as serving his wife. Servanthood is what is demanded, and it is servanthood that works.

Here's a quick Bible story. There was this woman named Abigail who was married to this idiot named "Idiot" *(I Samuel 25)*. Well, his name was Nabal which means "fool." Why would a mother name her son this? Who knows! Well, it seemed that King David wanted to pass through Nabal's property one day and sent to ask permission. The king didn't need permission, but he was a servant king. Nabal said something like, "You're not welcome here, You who are pretending to be a king." David was understandably angry. And as was the pattern of the Old Testament, David decided to slaughter Nabal, his family, his herds, his crops, and everything else belonging to him. Abigail intervened for her husband. She sent gifts to David and later went herself to bow down before the king. She said something like, "My husband is an idiot, that's probably why his momma named him idiot. But … he's my husband. Please spare him." Abigail is lifted up as one of the most beautiful women of the Bible because she put all of her energies into protecting her husband.

Servanthood works! It's what makes you beautiful. Practice servanthood in your home.

Practice Smooching. Do you remember when you couldn't keep your lips off of each other? You made everyone sick by kissing in public, in private, whenever and wherever you pleased. You need to pick up this habit again. If you cannot smooch, there are some ill feelings in your life that you haven't resolved. And, the lack of smooching may send a signal to your children that you are not as in love as you used to be. So, smooch a lot in front of your kids. It'll gross them out. But it will make you happy and it will provide them security in their own home.

Here's what you do. Make it a point to smooch in front of your kids at least once a day. They will say "Ooooh, gross." That just means you're doing it right. And if they ever say, "Get a room!" and know what that means, then really gross them out by grabbing your mates hand and marching back to the bedroom.

Your children need to see a healthy marriage modeled in their presence. Spend time taking care of your children's needs in this area. The benefits for your marriage will increase dramatically.

Legacy Marker #3 – The Marriage Champion

A marriage champion is one who constantly lifts up marriage as the best lifestyle. The champion celebrates his/ her own marriage and the marriage milestones of others.

Especially when your children get married, celebrate every anniversary with them through cards, phone calls, anything that tells them you are proud of them. Brag to your children about the other married couples you know and how well they are doing. When someone celebrates a 25th or 50th anniversary, let your children share in the cards or gifts you give to those beautiful couples. Tell your kids that they have to throw you a party on your 25th and 50th anniversaries. We did.

Our kids knew they had to throw us a 25th or Silver anniversary party. We reminded them often. We also told them they had to change our diapers when we get too old to take care of ourselves. But that's another story. Two or three years before our 25th, we stopped talking about the party they were supposed to organize for us. We knew that our two older kids would still be in high school, probably not making any money at all, and our youngest would still be in elementary school. We resigned ourselves to having a very small party. But one night, after evening services at our church, we were told that we needed to go to the fellowship room because "something happened." Nervously, we went. When we entered the room, many of our friends shouted "Surprise!" It turns out our kids invited as many of our friends as they could, AND they asked all of the attendees to pitch in for the refreshments. We were never more proud of our kids. I'm really looking forward to our 50th.

Today, my daughter is nearing her 1st wedding anniversary and my son is nearing his 7th. Though both live far away from us, we will send a card and make a call to help them celebrate these early milestones.

Legacy Marker #4 – The Virtual "Wall of Fame"

On the front page of our monthly newsletter we have a "Wall of Fame" on which we write the names and anniversaries of those celebrating their marriage that month. Usually, friends or family will send a donation to our non-profit organization in their honor. For that month, several thousands of our readers will know of those special couples and how many years they have been together. It's amazing.

Make a virtual "Wall of Fame" for your children. Constantly tell them about the anniversaries of well-known couples, especially the 25th and 50th anniversaries. Cut out newspaper articles or magazine spreads that celebrate and honor marriage. Send stories to your children of couples who struggled, but made it, through difficult circumstances. Encourage them to watch movies that honor marriage. Let them see that any couple can overcome any bad situation in life. Your "Wall of Fame" can act as a catalyst to keep your children from leaving when their own marriages suffer a bit.

Legacy Marker #5 –
"The Story of Our Marriage"

I believe all couples should write down their legacy for their children. For those younger married couples, write down the kind of legacy you want to leave for your children. Then get busy to make sure you practice a healthy marriage in front of them. For those older married couples, start accumulating stories from your marriage that will help your kids. Here are some suggestions on what you can include:

- What was so special about the mate you chose to live the rest of your life with?
- What were some of the beautiful moments early in your marriage?
- What were some of the difficulties you overcame that brought you closer together?
- How blessed was your marriage when each child entered the picture?
- What was the most difficult situation you had to overcome?

- When did you know for sure that your marriage would last "as long as you both shall live?"
- MORE MORE MORE

Write out this document so your children will benefit from your marriage for years to come. Give it to them early or leave it in your will. This could be one of the greatest gifts you could ever give your children. Put a lot of thought into it. Then let the love flow from your heart, through the pen, onto the paper, and into the hearts of your children. Your legacy will be a blessing to all who read it.

THE
SOVIET
SISTERS

Also by Anika Scott

The German Heiress